The Ultimate Christmas Guitar Songbook

ISBN-13: 978-1-4234-3195-4

HAL•LEONARD®
CORPORATION

7777 W. BLUEMOUND RD. P.O. BOX 13819 MILWAUKEE, WI 53213

Visit Hal Leonard Online at
www.halleonard.com

The Ultimate Christmas Guitar Songbook

Happy Xmas
(War Is Over)

Words and Music by John Lennon and Yoko Ono

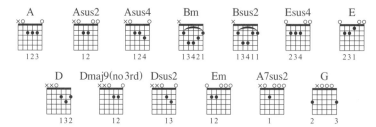

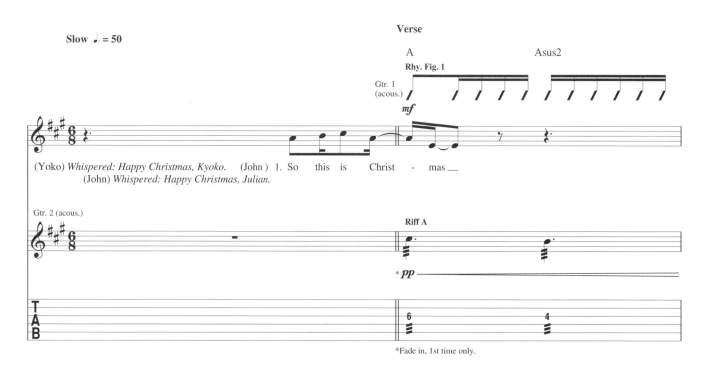

Slow ♩. = 50

Verse

(Yoko) *Whispered: Happy Christmas, Kyoko.*   (John) 1. So   this   is   Christ - mas __
          (John) *Whispered: Happy Christmas, Julian.*

Gtr. 2 (acous.)

Fade in, 1st time only.

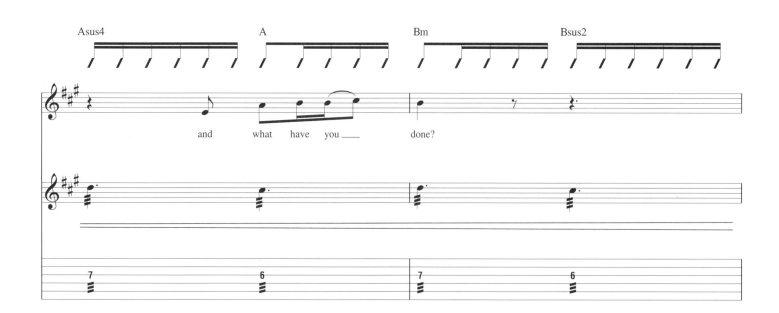

and   what   have   you __   done?

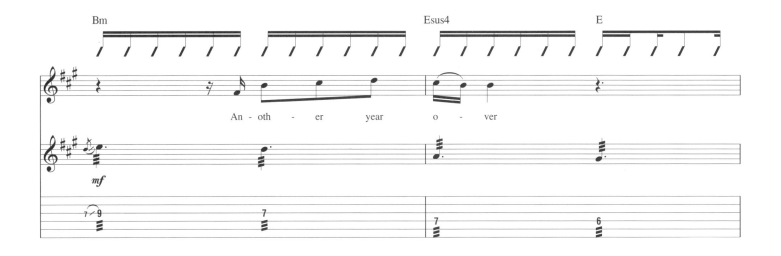

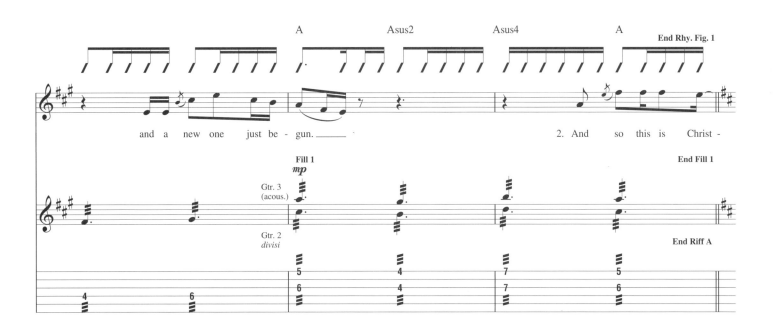

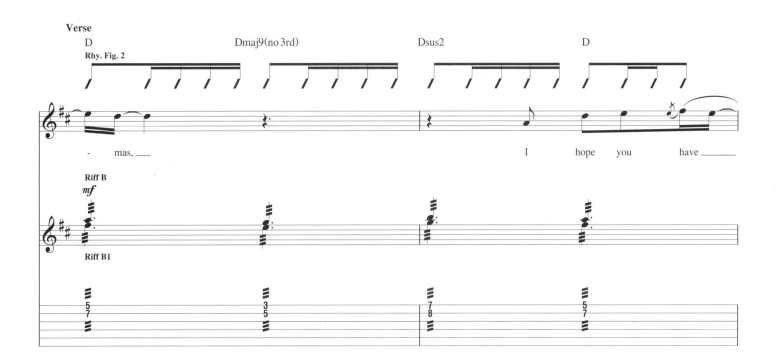

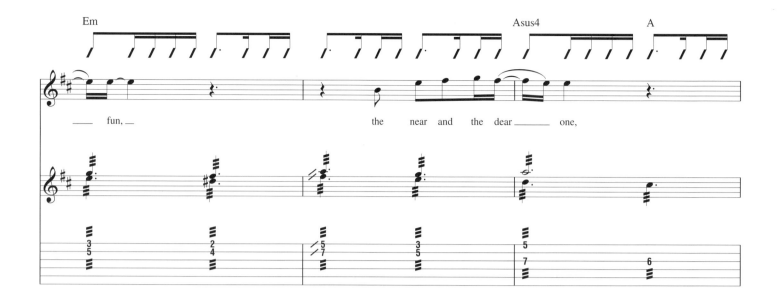

fun, ___ the near and the dear ___ one,

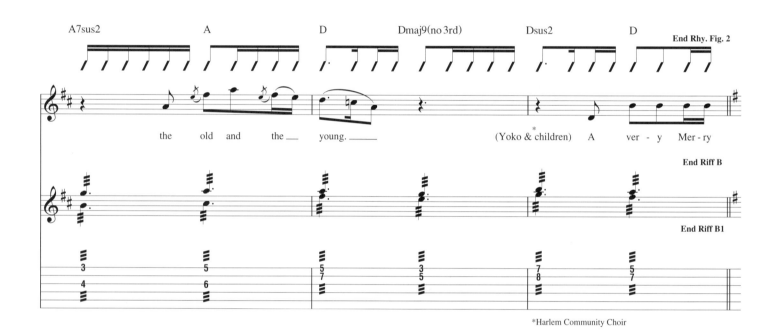

the old and the ___ young. ___ (Yoko & children) A ver - y Mer - ry

*Harlem Community Choir

Chorus

Christ - mas ___ and a hap - py New Year.

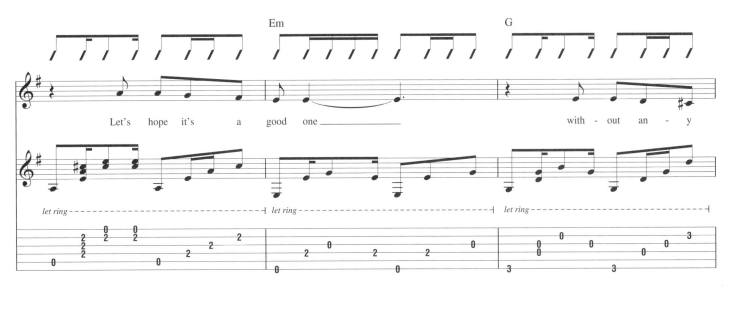

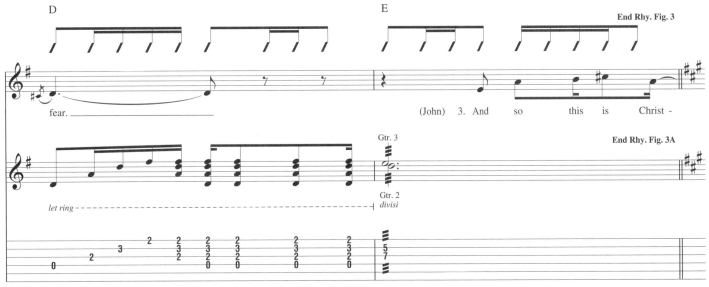

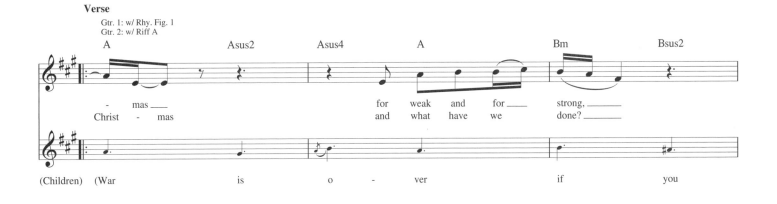

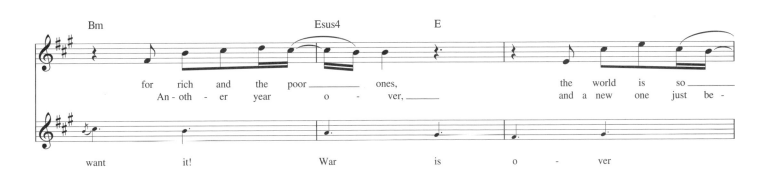

Jingle-Bell Rock

Words and Music by Joe Beal and Jim Boothe

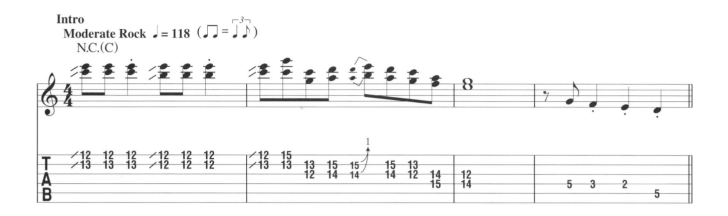

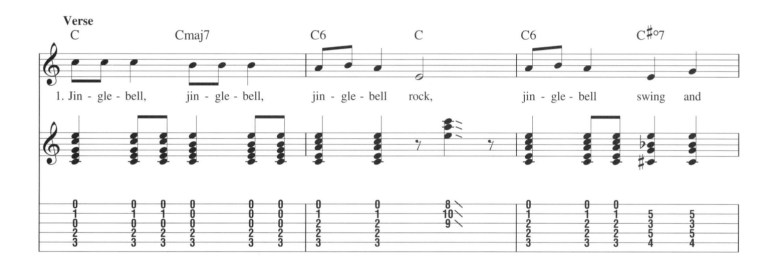

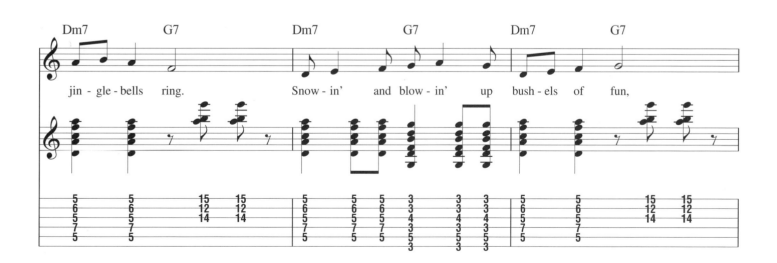

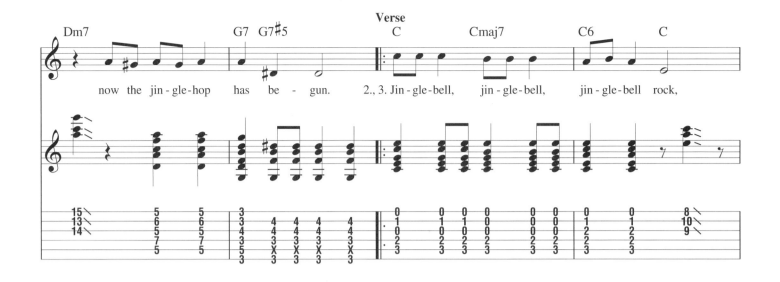

now the jin-gle-hop has be - gun. 2., 3. Jin-gle-bell, jin-gle-bell, jin-gle-bell rock,

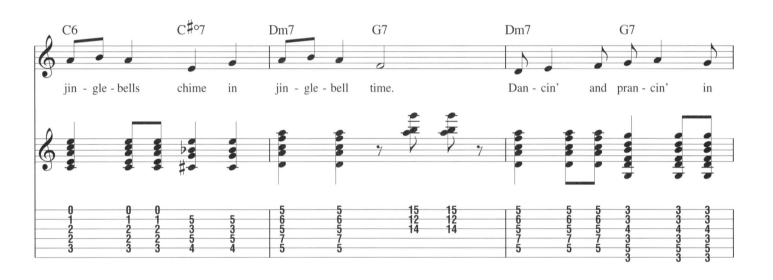

jin-gle-bells chime in jin-gle-bell time. Dan-cin' and pran-cin' in

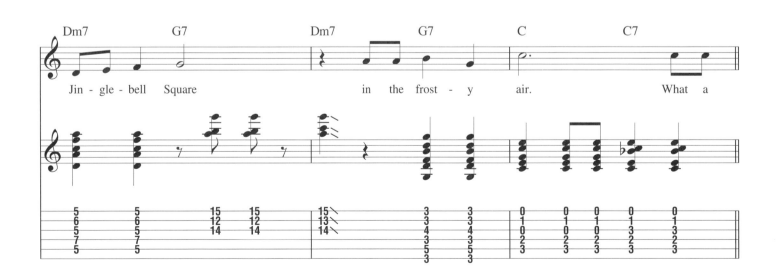

Jin-gle-bell Square in the frost-y air. What a

Bridge

bright time, it's the right time to rock the night a-

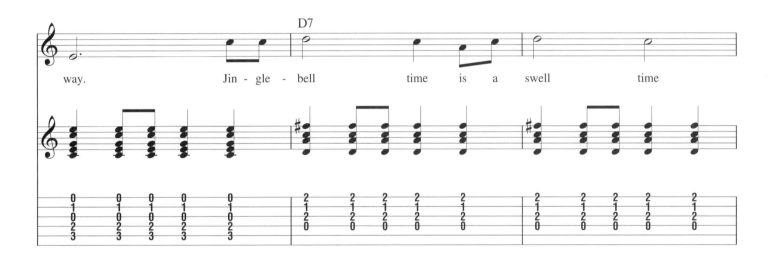

way. Jin - gle - bell time is a swell time

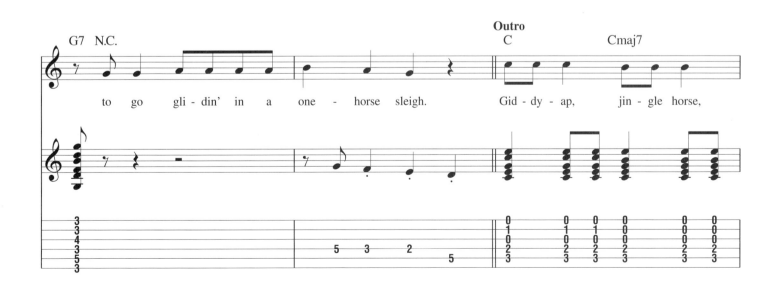

to go gli - din' in a one - horse sleigh. Gid - dy - ap, jin - gle horse,

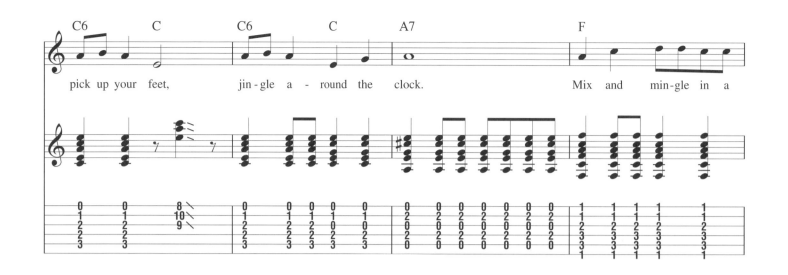

pick up your feet, jin-gle a - round the clock. Mix and min-gle in a

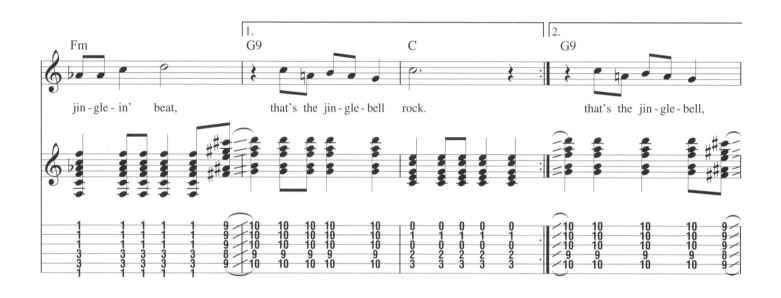

jin-gle - in' beat, that's the jin-gle-bell rock. that's the jin-gle - bell,

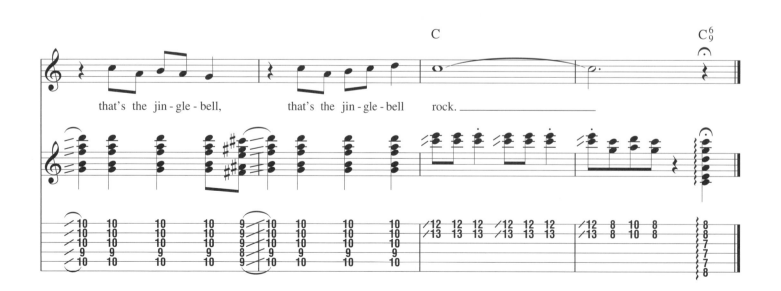

that's the jin-gle - bell, that's the jin-gle-bell rock.

Little Saint Nick

Words and Music by Brian Wilson and Mike Love

Tune down 1/2 step:
(low to high) E♭-A♭-D♭-G♭-B♭-E♭

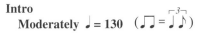

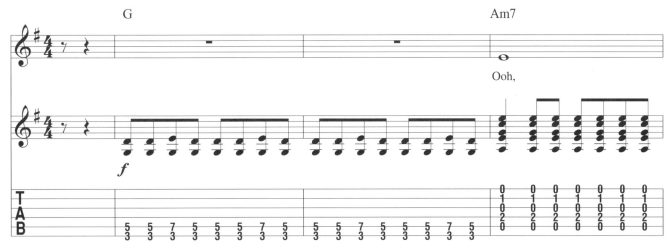

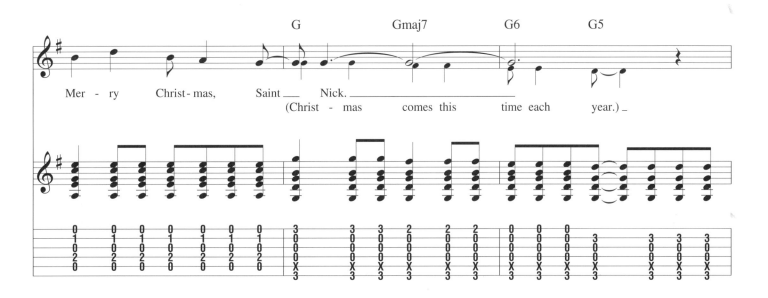

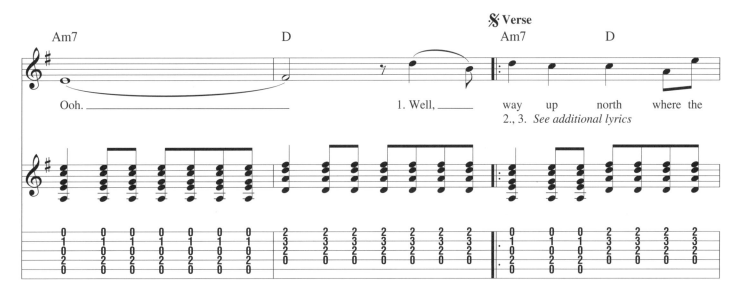

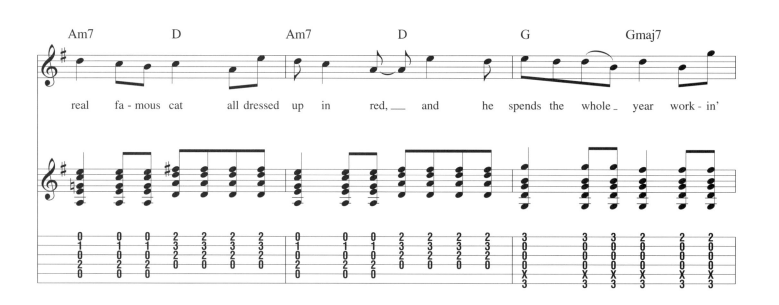

To Coda ⊕

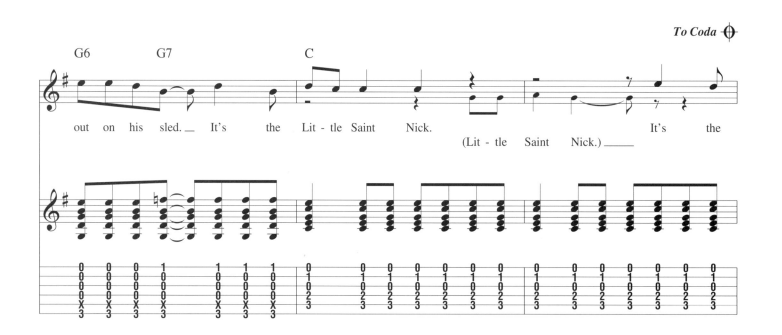

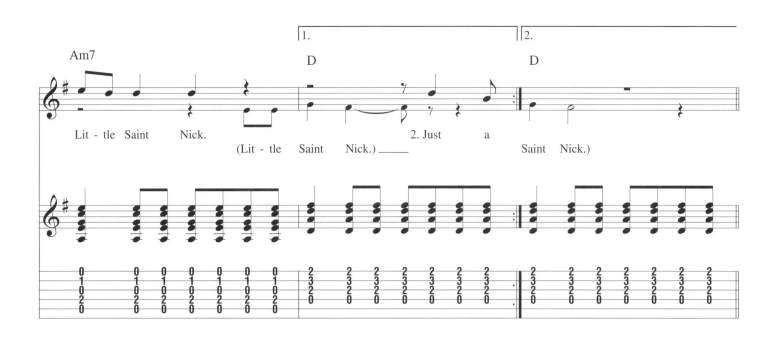

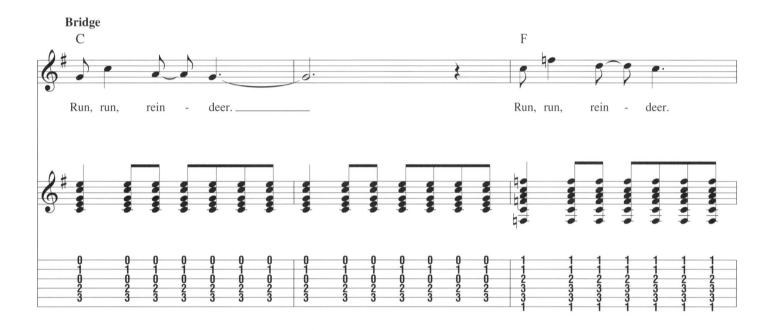

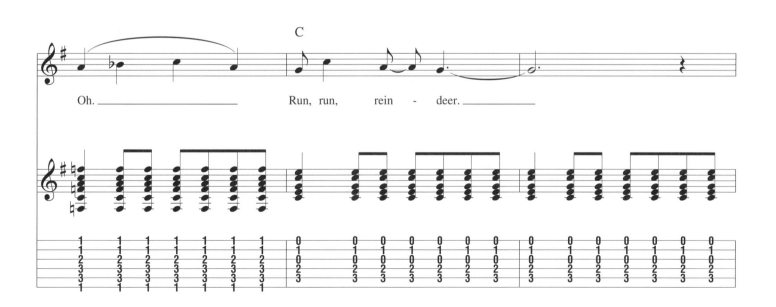

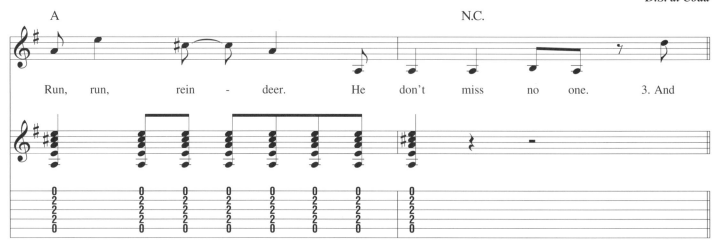

Run, run, rein - deer. He don't miss no one. 3. And

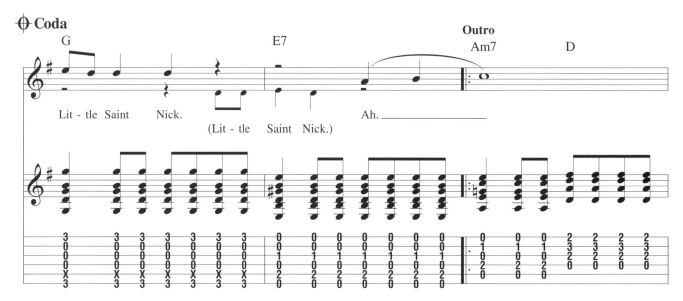

Lit - tle Saint Nick.
(Lit - tle Saint Nick.)
Ah.

Repeat and fade

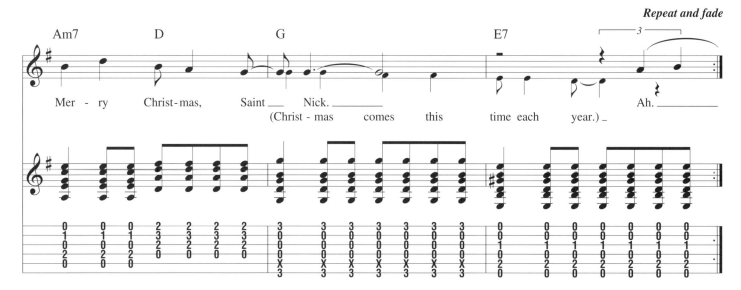

Mer - ry Christ-mas, Saint Nick.
(Christ - mas comes this time each year.)
Ah.

Additional Lyrics

2. Just a little bobsled, we call it Old Saint Nick,
   But she'll walk a toboggan with a four-speed stick.
   She's candy apple red with a ski for a wheel,
   And when Santa hits the gas, man, just watch her peel.

3. And haulin' through the snow at a fright'nin' speed
   With a half a dozen deer with Rudy to lead.
   He's gotta wear his goggles 'cause the snow really flies,
   And he's cruisin' ev'ry pad with a little surprise.

Pretty Paper

Words and Music by Willie Nelson

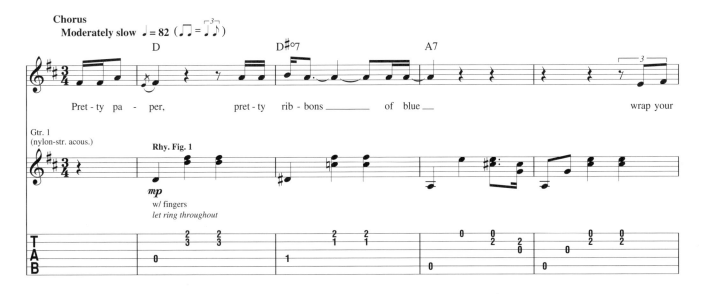

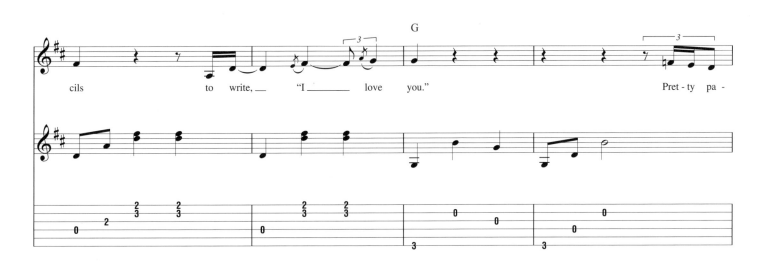

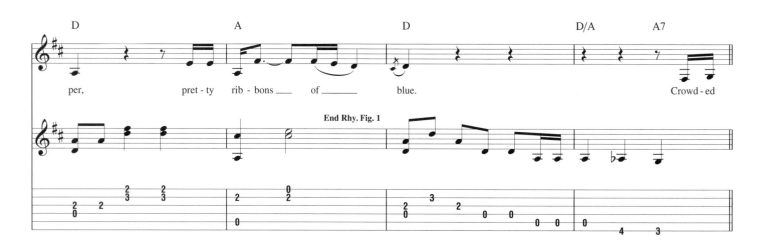

per, pret-ty rib-bons ___ of ___ blue.   Crowd-ed

End Rhy. Fig. 1

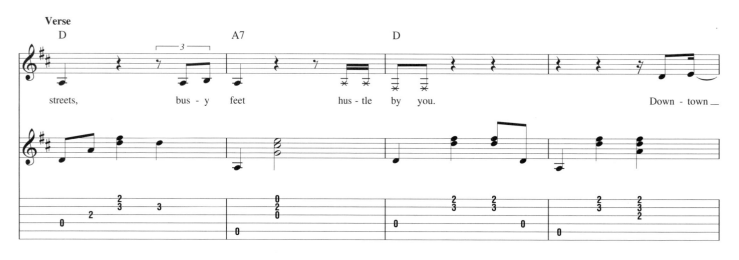

Verse

streets, bus-y feet hus-tle by you.   Down-town ___

___ shop-pers, ___ Christ-mas ___ is nigh. ___   And there he

sits all a-lone on ___ the side-walk,

*Played as even eighth-notes.

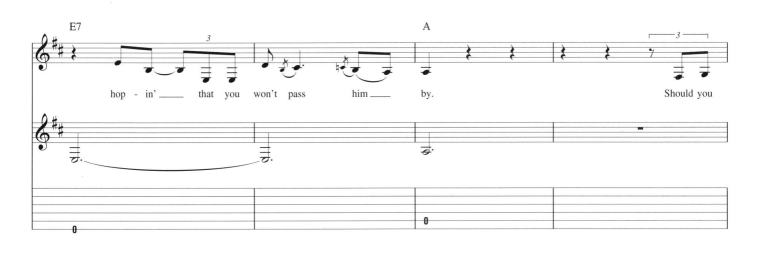

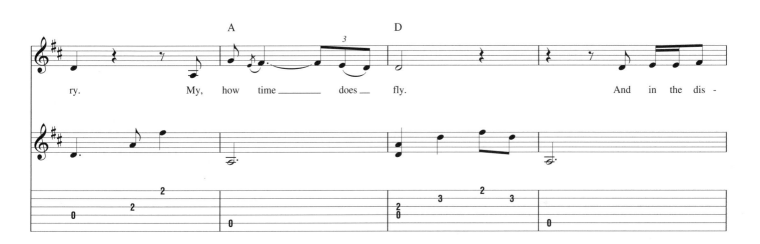

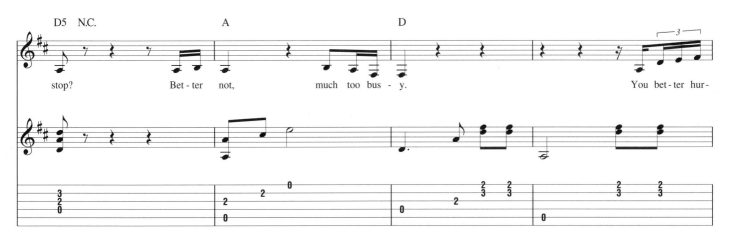

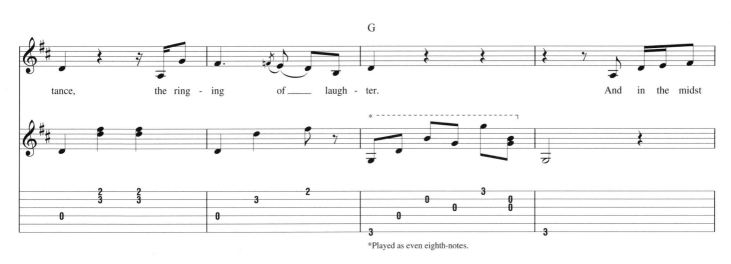

*Played as even eighth-notes.

Chorus

Gtr. 1: w/ Rhy. Fig. 1

*Played as even eighth-notes.

**As before.

Rockin' Around the Christmas Tree

Music and Lyrics by Johnny Marks

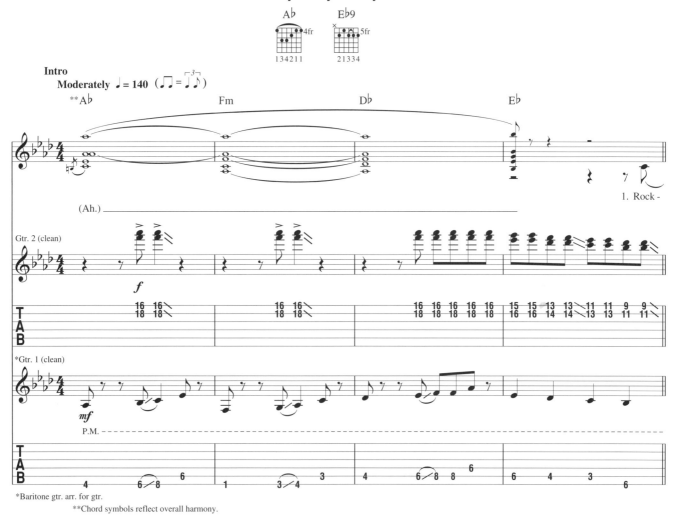

Mis-tle-toe hung _ where you can see _ ev -'ry cou -ple tri -es to stop. _ Rock-

Oo. _____

P.M. --------------------------------

End Riff A

Gtr. 1: w/ Riff A (1st 4 meas.)
Gtr. 2 tacet

Gtr. 2: w/ Fill 1

-in' a -round _ the Christ-mas tree, _ let the Christ-mas spir -it ring. _

Oo. _____

Lat -er we'll have _ some pump -kin pie _ and we'll do some car -ol -ing.

Oo.) _____

Gtr. 2

Gtr. 1

P.M. --------------------------------

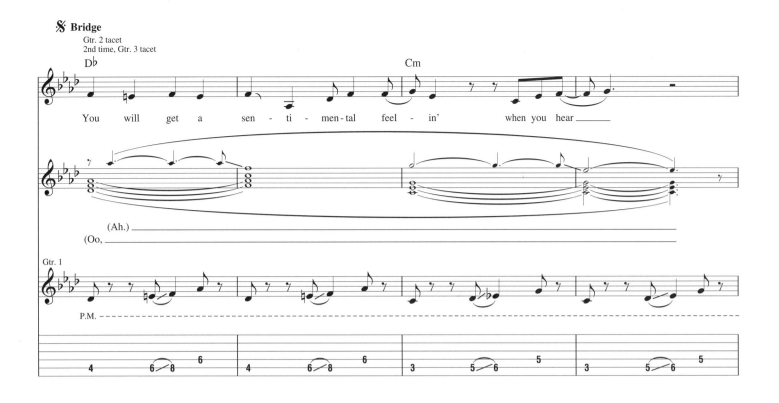

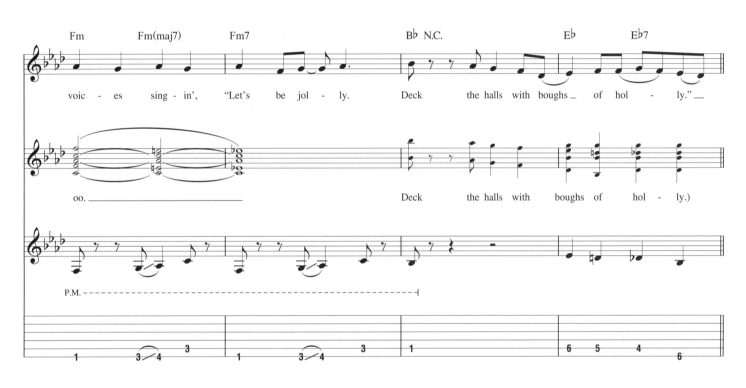

To Coda ⊕

Ev -'ry - one danc - in' mer - ri - ly in the new old fash - ion way.

Oo.)

*Gtr. 3

w/ dist.

*Tenor sax arr. for gtr.

Gtr. 2

Sax Solo

Gtr. 1

P.M. -

Voc. Fig. 1

(Ah.

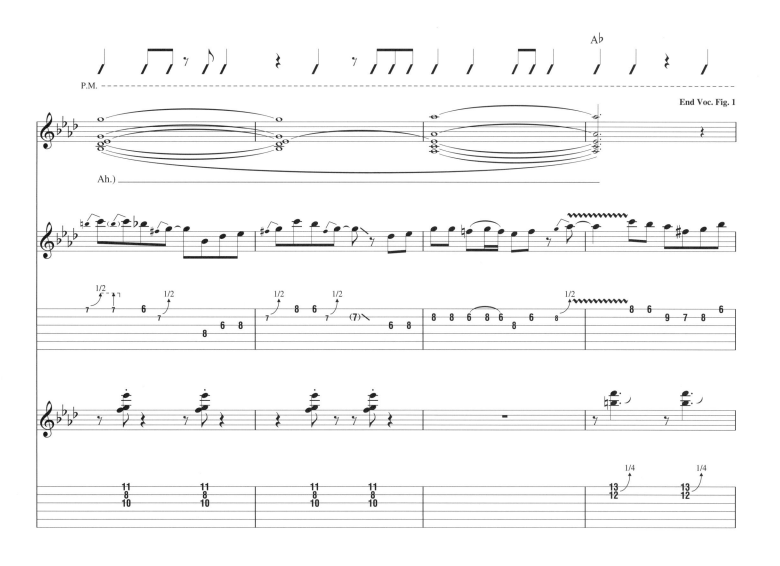

Coda

Wonderful Christmastime

Words and Music by Paul McCartney

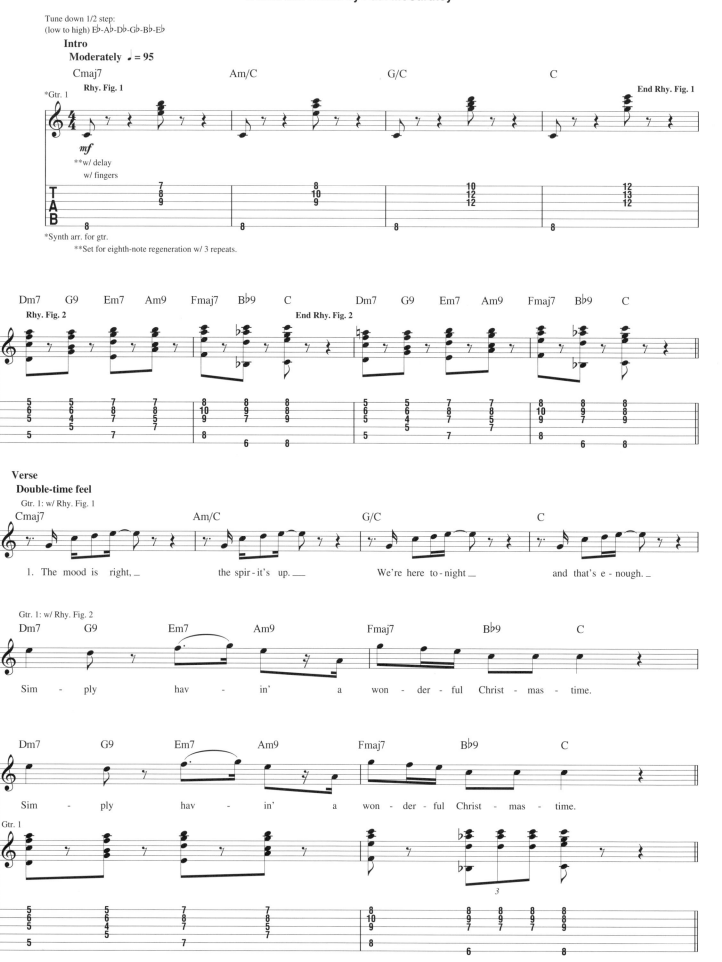

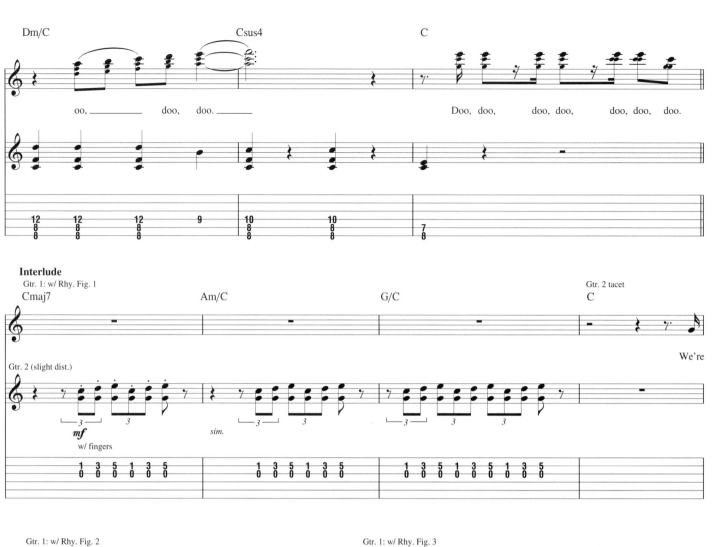

Interlude

Verse

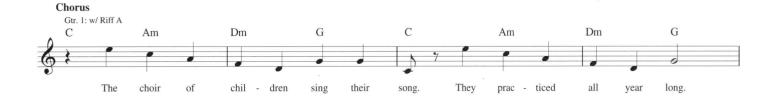

Chorus

Gtr. 1: w/ Riff A

| C | Am | Dm | G | C | Am | Dm | G |

The choir of chil - dren sing their song. They prac - ticed all year long.

| C | F/C | Dm7 | Cadd9 | | G | G7 |

Ding, dong, ding, dong, ding, dong, dong, dong, ding, dong, dong, dong, dong,
(Ding, dong, ding, dong, ding, dong, ding, dong, ding, dong, ding, dong, ding, dong, dong,

Gtr. 1

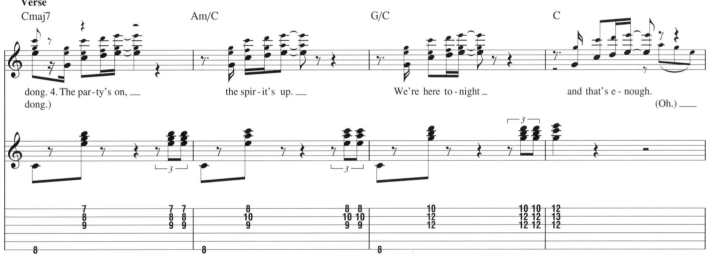

Verse

| Cmaj7 | Am/C | G/C | C |

dong. 4. The par-ty's on, __ the spir-it's up. __ We're here to-night __ and that's e - nough.
dong.) (Oh.) __

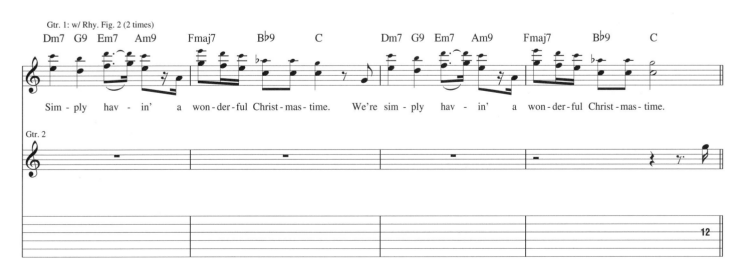

Gtr. 1: w/ Rhy. Fig. 2 (2 times)

| Dm7 G9 Em7 Am9 | Fmaj7 | B♭9 | C | Dm7 G9 Em7 Am9 | Fmaj7 | B♭9 | C |

Sim - ply hav - in' a won - der - ful Christ - mas - time. We're sim - ply hav - in' a won - der - ful Christ - mas - time.

Gtr. 2

Guitar Solo
w/ ad lib. vocals

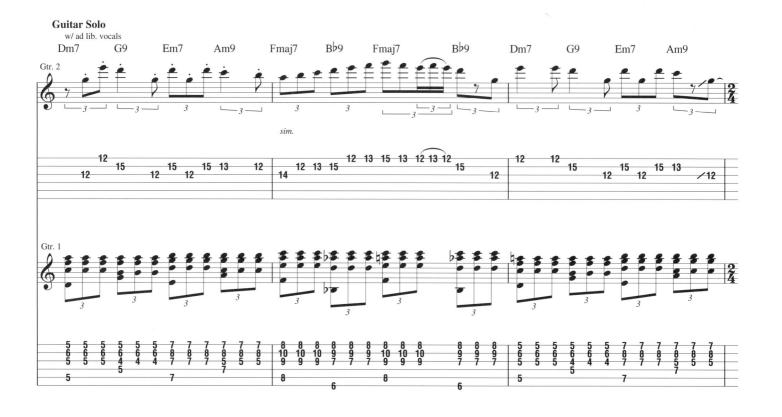

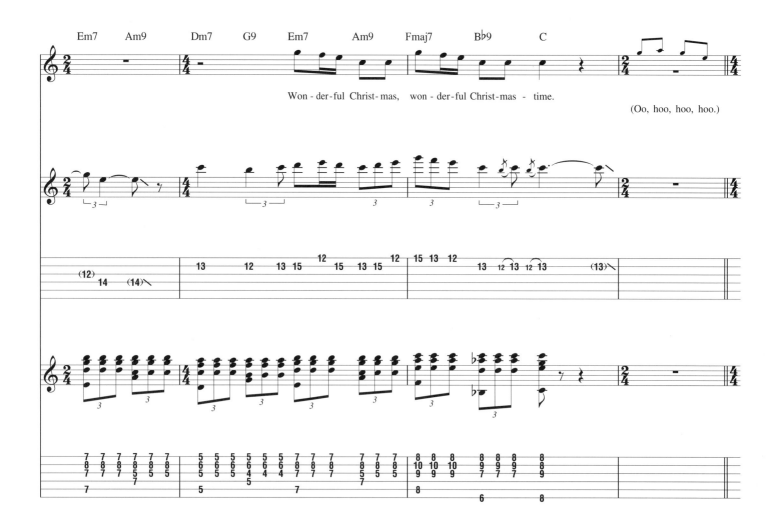

Won - der-ful Christ - mas, won - der-ful Christ - mas - time.

(Oo, hoo, hoo, hoo.)

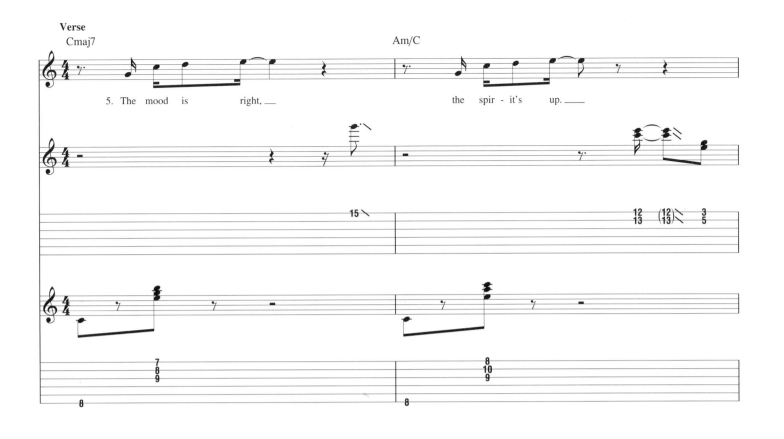

Verse

Cmaj7   Am/C

5. The mood is right, ___ the spir - it's up. ___

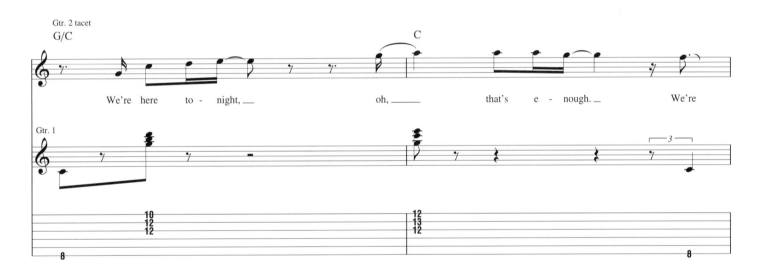

Gtr. 2 tacet

G/C   C

We're here to - night, ___ oh, ___ that's e - nough. ___ We're

Gtr. 1

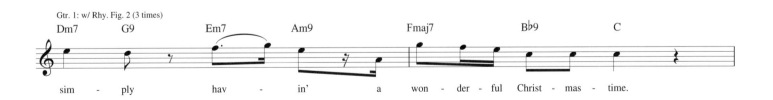

Gtr. 1: w/ Rhy. Fig. 2 (3 times)

Dm7   G9   Em7   Am9   Fmaj7   B♭9   C

sim - ply hav - in' a won - der - ful Christ - mas - time.

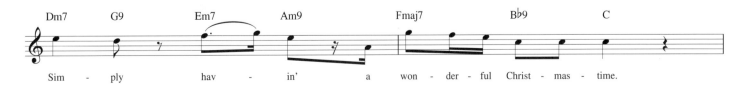

Dm7   G9   Em7   Am9   Fmaj7   B♭9   C

Sim - ply hav - in' a won - der - ful Christ - mas - time.

Sim - ply hav - in' a won - der - ful Christ - mas - time.

Outro

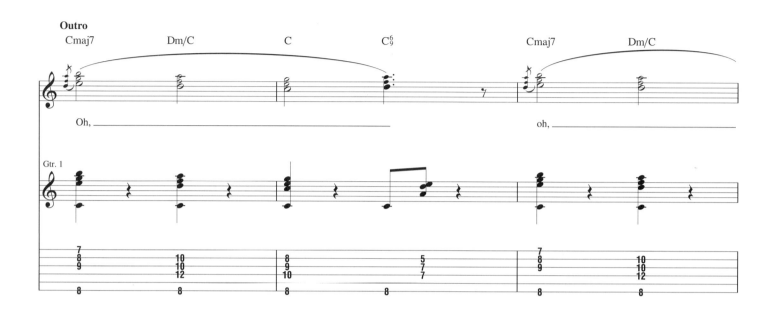

Oh, _____ oh, _____

Gtr. 1

— (Won - der - ful Christ - mas - time, Christ - mas - time. Christ - mas - time.)

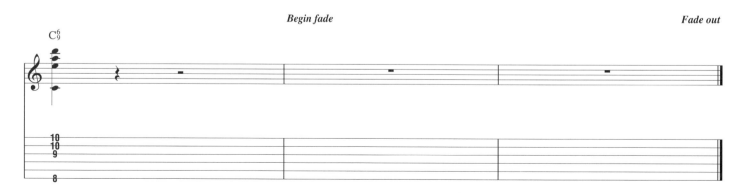

Begin fade   *Fade out*

Auld Lang Syne

Words by Robert Burns
Traditional Scottish Melody

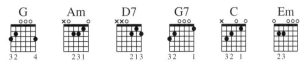

Strum Pattern: 3, 4
Pick Pattern: 2, 4

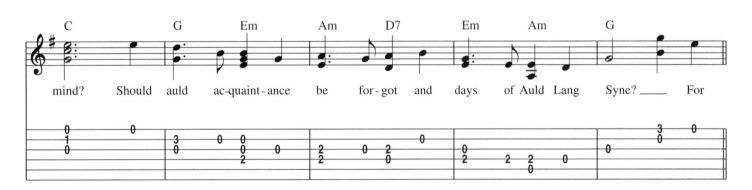

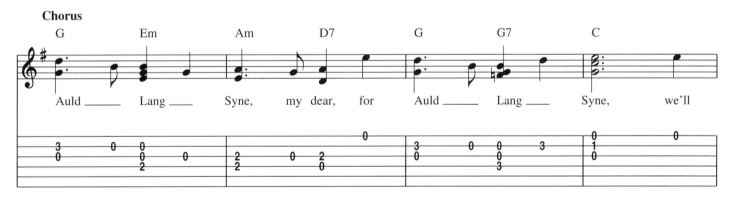

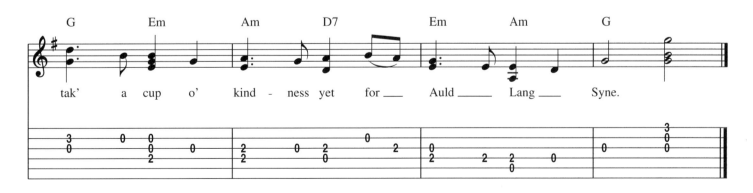

All Through the Night

Welsh Folksong

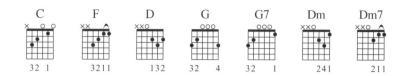

Strum Pattern: 3
Pick Pattern: 4

Verse
Moderately

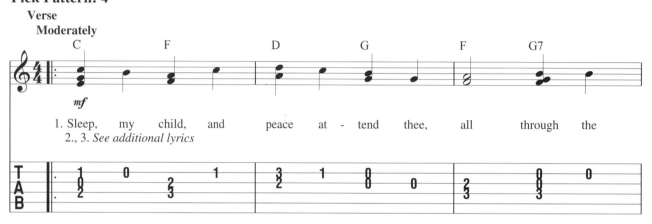

mf

1. Sleep, my child, and peace at - tend thee, all through the
2., 3. *See additional lyrics*

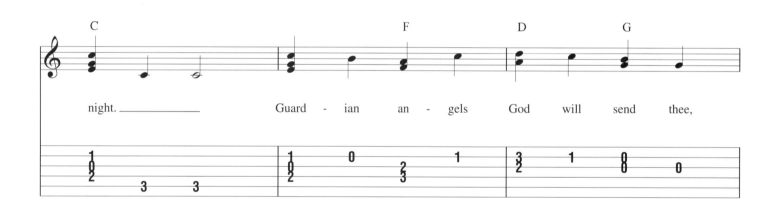

night. _____ Guard - ian an - gels God will send thee,

all through the night. _____ Soft, the drow - sy

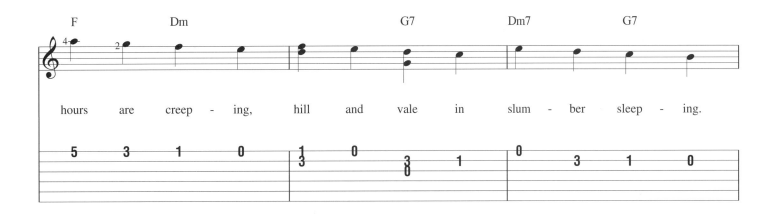

hours are creep - ing, hill and vale in slum - ber sleep - ing.

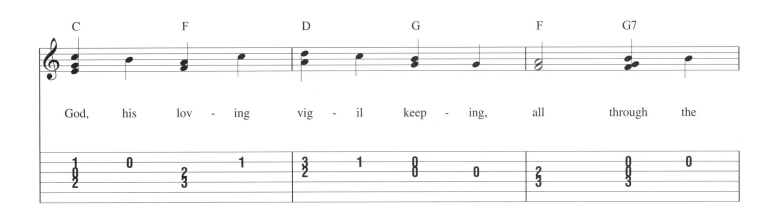

God, his lov - ing vig - il keep - ing, all through the

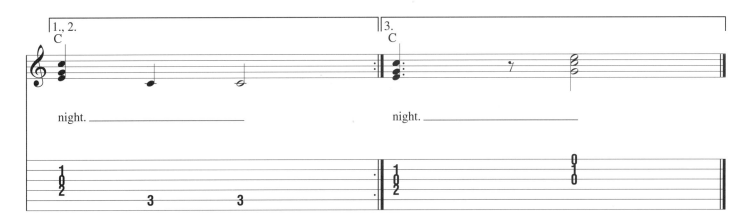

night. _____ night. _____

Additional Lyrics

2. While the moon, her watch is keeping,
   All through the night.
   While the weary world is sleeping,
   All through the night.
   Through your dreams you're swiflty stealing,
   Visions of delight revealing,
   Christmas time is so appealing,
   All through the night.

3. You, my God, a babe of wonder,
   All through the night.
   Dreams you can't break from thunder,
   All through the night.
   Children's dreams cannot be broken.
   Life is but a lovely token.
   Christmas should be softly spoken,
   All through the night.

Angels We Have Heard on High

Traditional French Carol
Translated by James Chadwick

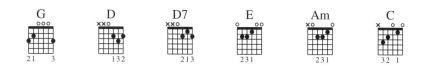

Strum Pattern: 6
Pick Pattern: 6

Verse
Moderately

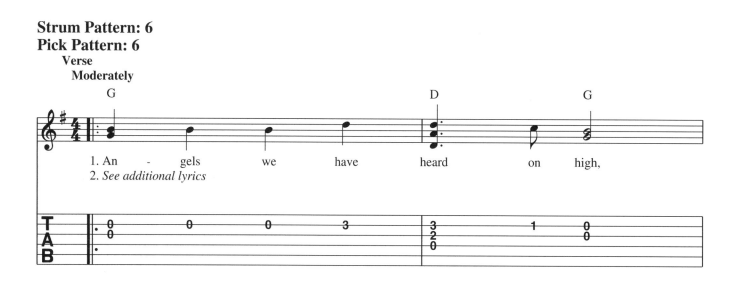

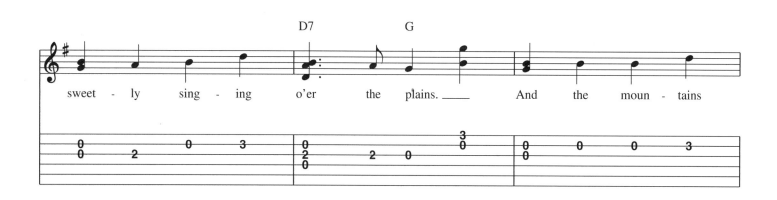

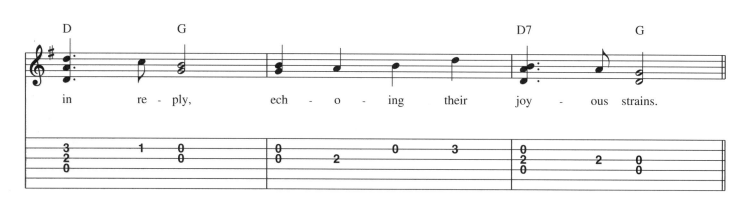

Chorus

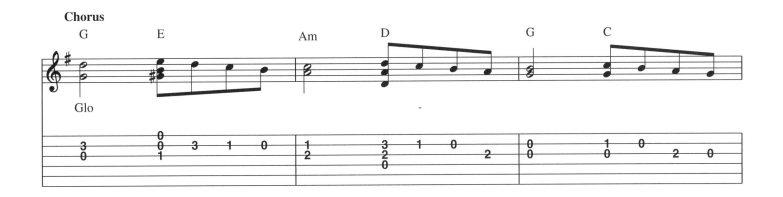

Glo -

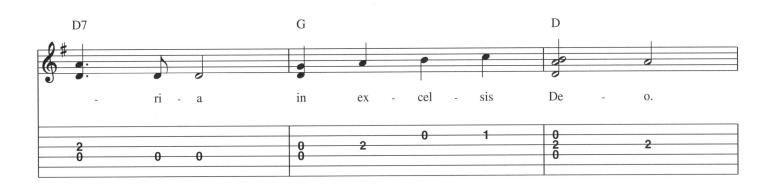

- ri - a in ex - cel - sis De - o.

Glo - ri - a

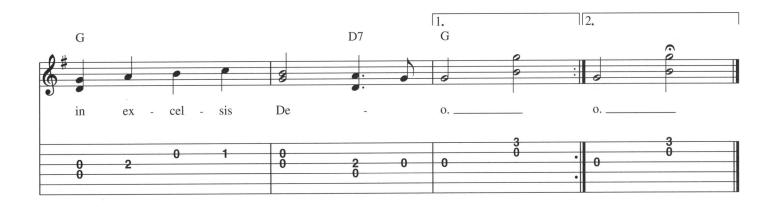

in ex - cel - sis De - o. _____ o. _____

Additional Lyrics

2. Shepherds why this jubilee?
   Why your joyous strains prolong?
   What the gladsome tidings be
   Which inspire your heavenly song?

Away in a Manger

Words by John T. McFarland (v.3)
Music by James R. Murray

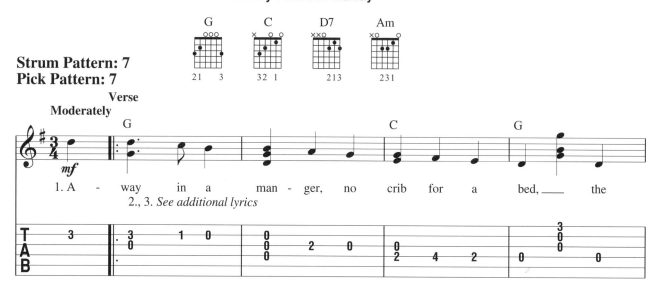

Strum Pattern: 7
Pick Pattern: 7

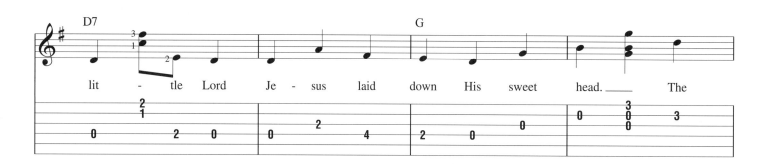

1. A - way in a man - ger, no crib for a bed, ___ the
2., 3. *See additional lyrics*

lit - tle Lord Je - sus laid down His sweet head. ___ The

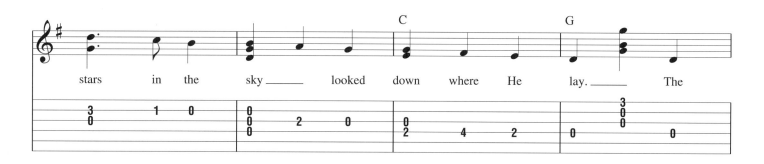

stars in the sky ___ looked down where He lay. ___ The

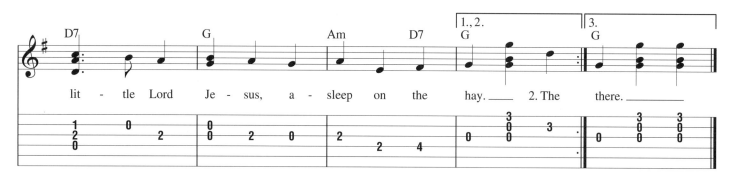

lit - tle Lord Je - sus, a - sleep on the hay. ___ 2. The there. ___

Additional Lyrics

2. The cattle are lowing, the baby awakes,
   But little Lord Jesus, no crying He makes.
   I love thee, Lord Jesus, look down from the sky
   And stay by my cradle 'til morning is nigh.

3. Be near me, Lord Jesus, I ask Thee to stay
   Close by me forever, and love me, I pray.
   Bless all the dear children in Thy tender care,
   And fit us for heaven to live with Thee there.

Deck the Hall

Traditional Welsh Carol

Strum Pattern: 4, 6
Pick Pattern: 5, 6

Verse
Gaily

1. Deck the hall with boughs of hol-ly; fa, la, la, la, la, la, la, la, la.
2., 3. *See additional lyrics*

'Tis the sea-son to be jol-ly; fa, la, la, la, la, la, la, la, la.

Don we now our gay ap-par-el; fa, la, la, la, la, la, la, la, la. ____

Troll the an-cient yule-tide car-ol; fa, la, la, la, la, la, la, la, la. ____ la, la, la. ____

Additional Lyrics

2. See the blazing yule before us;
Fa, la, la, la, la, la, la, la, la.
Strike the harp and join the chorus;
Fa, la, la, la, la, la, la, la, la.
Follow me in merry measure;
Fa, la, la, la, la, la, la, la, la, la.
While I tell of Yuletide treasure;
Fa, la, la, la, la, la, la, la, la.

3. Fast away the old year passes;
Fa, la, la, la, la, la, la, la, la.
Hail the new ye lads and lasses;
Fa, la, la, la, la, la, la, la, la.
Sing we joyous, all together;
Fa, la, la, la, la, la, la, la, la.
Heedless of the wind and weather;
Fa, la, la, la, la, la, la, la, la.

Christmas Is

Lyrics by Spence Maxwell
Music by Percy Faith

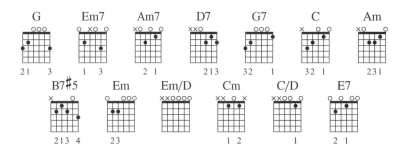

Strum Pattern: 3, 4
Pick Pattern: 3

Intro
Moderately slow

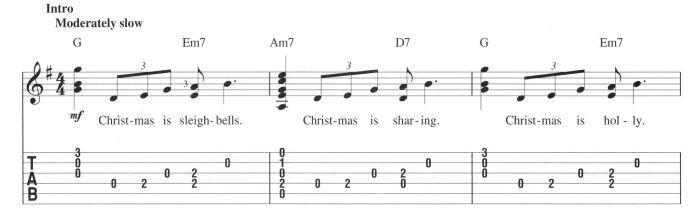

Verse

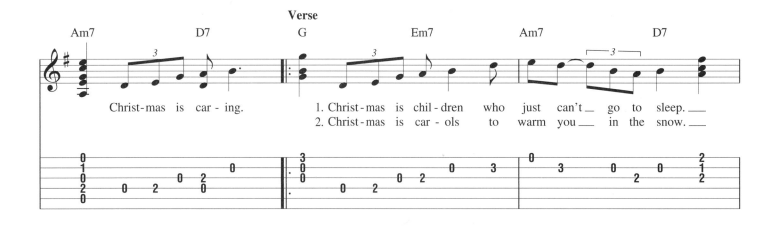

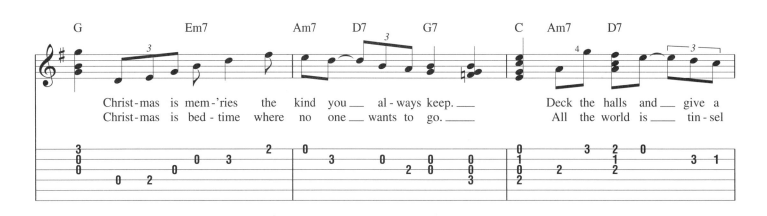

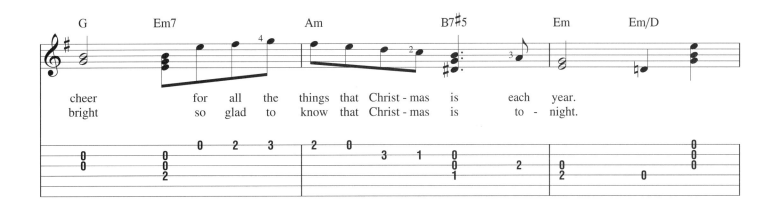

cheer   for   all   the   things   that   Christ - mas   is   each   year.

bright   so   glad   to   know   that   Christ - mas   is   to - night.

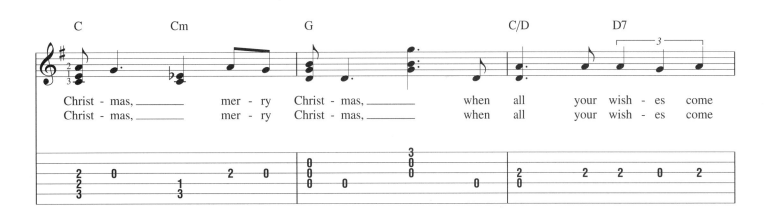

Christ - mas, _____   mer - ry   Christ - mas, _____   when   all   your   wish - es   come

Christ - mas, _____   mer - ry   Christ - mas, _____   when   all   your   wish - es   come

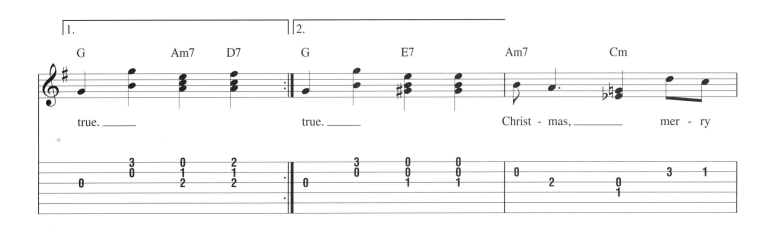

1.

true. _____

2.

true. _____   Christ - mas, _____   mer - ry

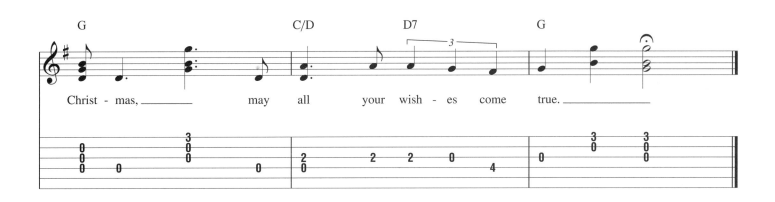

Christ - mas, _____   may   all   your   wish - es   come   true. _____

Christmas Time Is Here

from A CHARLIE BROWN CHRISTMAS

Words by Lee Mendelson
Music by Vince Guaraldi

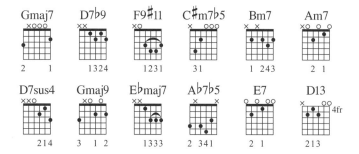

Strum Pattern: 7, 8
Pick Pattern: 7, 8

Intro
Slowly

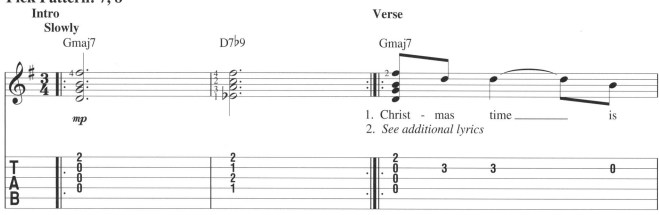

1. Christ - mas time _____ is
2. *See additional lyrics*

here, hap - pi - ness _____ and cheer. Fun for all _____ that

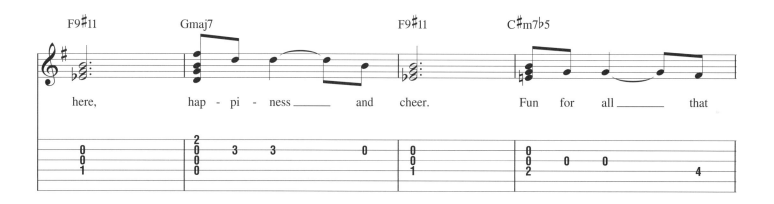

chil - dren call _____ their fa - v'rite time of year. _____ share. _____

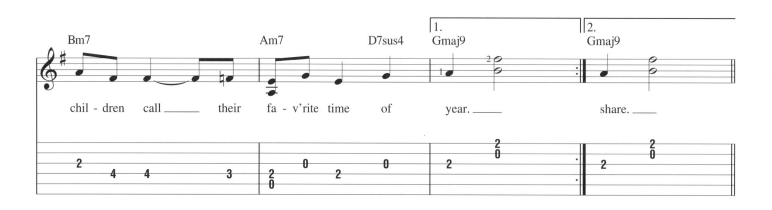

Bridge

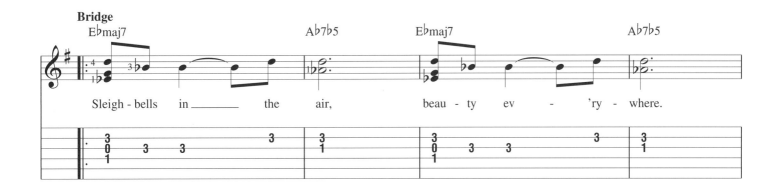

Sleigh - bells in _____ the air, beau - ty ev - 'ry - where.

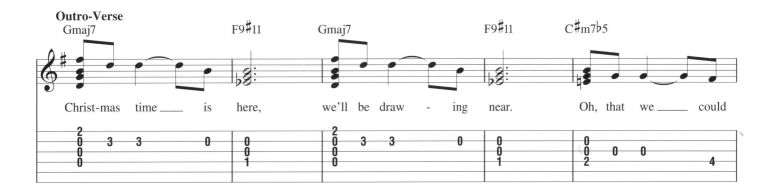

Yule - tide by _____ the fire - side _____ and joy - ful mem - 'ries there.

Outro-Verse

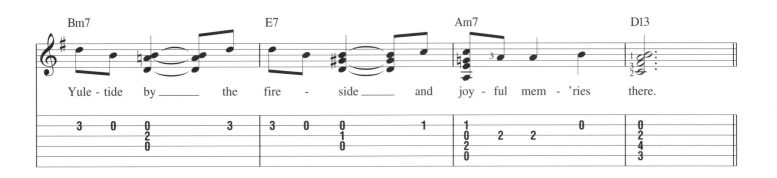

Christ-mas time ____ is here, we'll be draw - ing near. Oh, that we ____ could

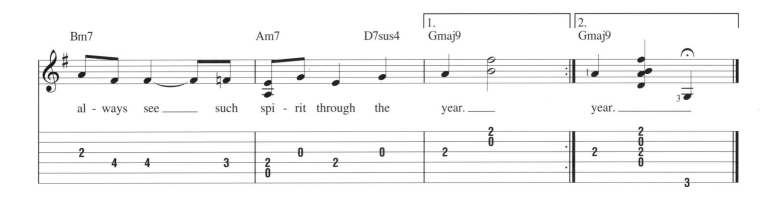

al - ways see ____ such spi - rit through the year. ____ year. ____

Additional Lyrics

2. Snowflakes in the air,
   Carols ev'rywhere.
   Olden times and ancient rhymes
   Of love and dreams to share.

The First Noël

17th Century English
Music from W. Sandys' *Christmas Carols*

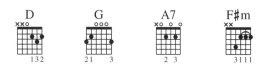

Strum Pattern: 7, 8
Pick Pattern: 8, 9

Verse
Moderately slow

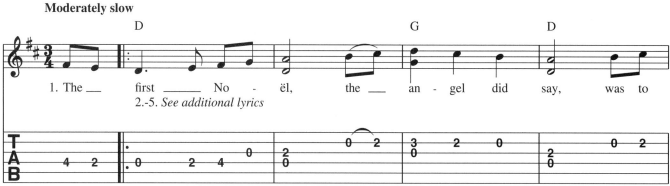

1. The first No - ël, the an - gel did say, was to
2.-5. *See additional lyrics*

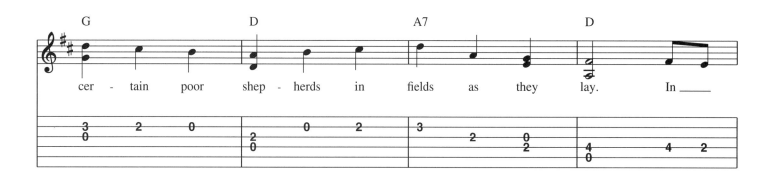

cer - tain poor shep - herds in fields as they lay. In

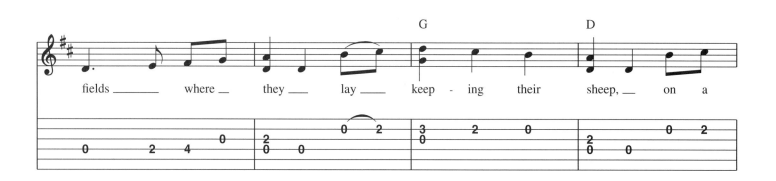

fields where they lay keep - ing their sheep, on a

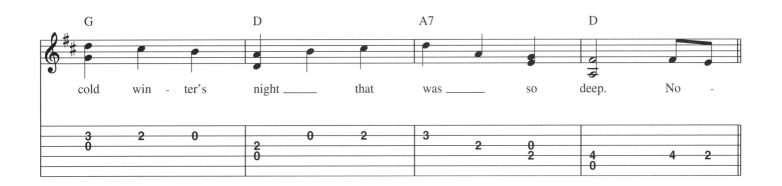

cold win - ter's night _____ that was _____ so deep. No -

Chorus

ël, _____ No - ël, No - ël, No - ël, _____

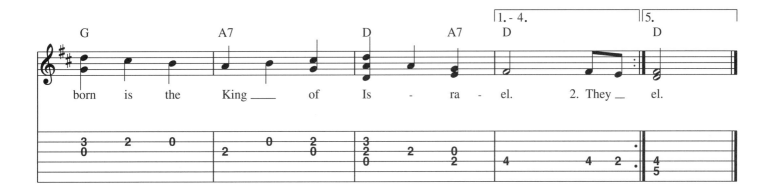

born is the King _____ of Is - ra - el. 2. They _ el.

Additional Lyrics

2. They looked up and saw a star
   Shining in the East, beyond them far.
   And to the earth it gave great light,
   And so it continued both day and night.

3. And by the light of that same star,
   Three wise man came from country far;
   To seek for a King was their intent,
   And to follow the star wherever it went.

4. This star drew nigh to the northwest,
   O'er Bethlehem it took its rest;
   And there it did both stop and stay,
   Right over the place where Jesus lay.

5. Then entered in those wise men three,
   Full reverently upon their knee;
   And offered there in His presence,
   Their gold and myrrh and frankincense.

Hard Candy Christmas

Words and Music by Carol Hall

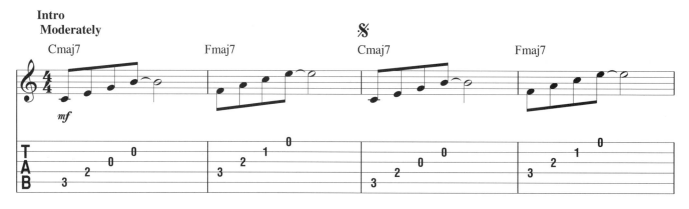

Strum Pattern: 6
Pick Pattern: 2

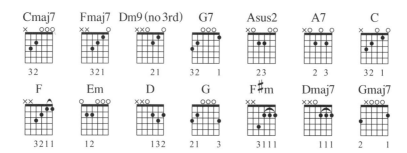

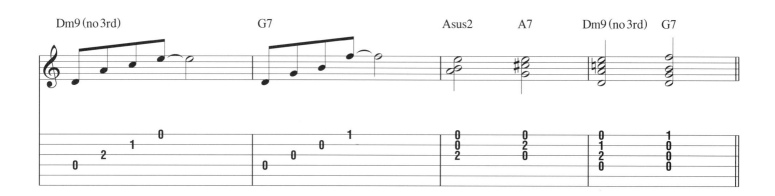

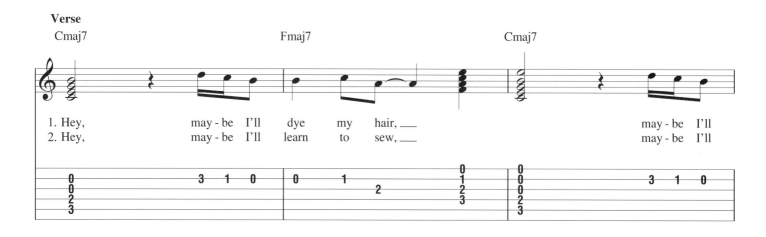

1. Hey, may-be I'll dye my hair, ___ may-be I'll
2. Hey, may-be I'll learn to sew, ___ may-be I'll

Jolly Old St. Nicholas

Traditional 19th Century American Carol

Strum Pattern: 4
Pick Pattern: 4

Verse
Brightly

1. Jol - ly old Saint Nich - o - las, lean your ear this way.

2., 3. *See additional lyrics*

Don't you tell a sin - gle soul what I'm going to say.

Christ - mas Eve is com - ing soon, now, you dear old man,

whis - per what you'll bring to me; tell me if you can. best.

Additional Lyrics

2. When the clock is striking twelve, when I'm fast asleep,
   Down the chimney broad and black, with your pack you'll creep.
   All the stockings you will find hanging in a row.
   Mine will be the shortest one, you'll be sure to know.

3. Johnny wants a pair of skates; Susy wants a sled.
   Nellie wants a picture book, yellow, blue and red.
   Now I think I'll leave to you what to give the rest.
   Choose for me, dear Santa Claus.
   You will know the best.

Hark! The Herald Angels Sing

Words by Charles Wesley
Altered by George Whitefield
Music by Felix Mendelssohn-Bartholdy
Arranged by William H. Cummings

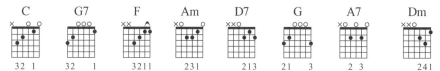

Strum Pattern: 3, 2
Pick Pattern: 3, 4

Verse
Joyfully

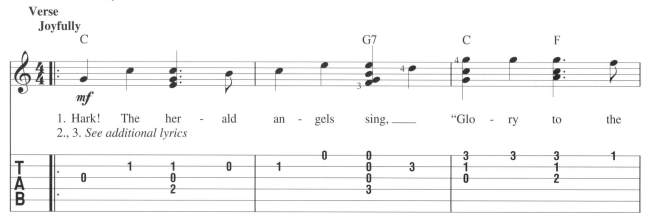

1. Hark! The her - ald an - gels sing, ____ "Glo - ry to the
2., 3. *See additional lyrics*

new - born King! Peace on earth, and mer - cy mild, _____

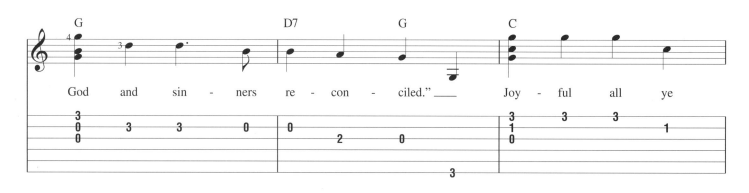

God and sin - ners re - con - ciled." ____ Joy - ful all ye

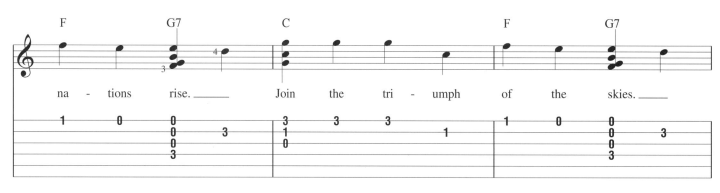

na - tions rise. ____ Join the tri - umph of the skies. ____

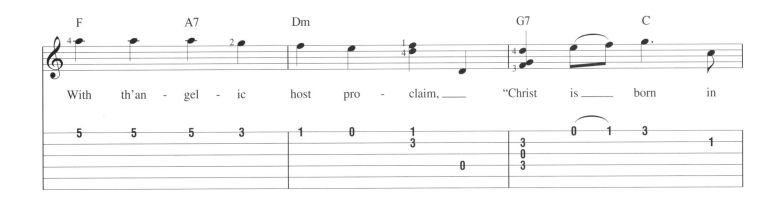

With th'an - gel - ic host pro - claim, ___ "Christ is ___ born in

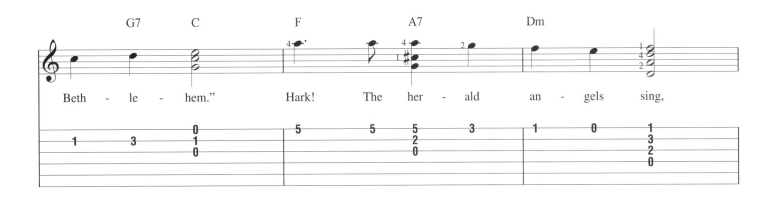

Beth - le - hem." Hark! The her - ald an - gels sing,

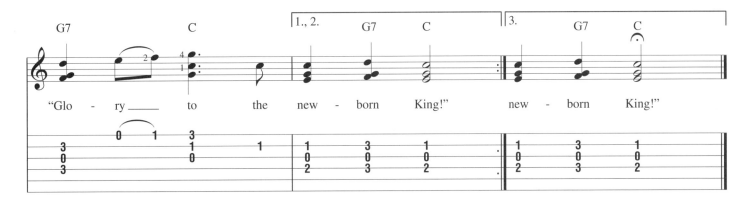

"Glo - ry ___ to the new - born King!" new - born King!"

Additional Lyrics

2. Christ, by highest heav'n adored,
Christ, the everlasting Lord;
Late in time behold Him come,
Offspring of the Virgin's womb.
Veil'd in flesh the Godhead see,
Hail th'Incarnate Deity.
Pleased as Man with man to dwell,
Jesus, our Emmanuel!
Hark! The herald angels sing,
"Glory to the newborn King!"

3. Mild, He lays His glory by,
Born that man no more may die.
Born to raise the sons of earth,
Born to give them second birth.
Ris'n with healing in His wings,
Light and life to all He brings.
Hail the Son of Righteousness!
Hail the heav'n-born Prince of Peace!
Hark! The herald angels sing,
"Glory to the newborn King!"

Here We Come A-Wassailing

Traditional

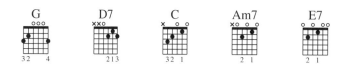

Strum Pattern: 8, 9
Pick Pattern: 7, 9

Verse
Brightly

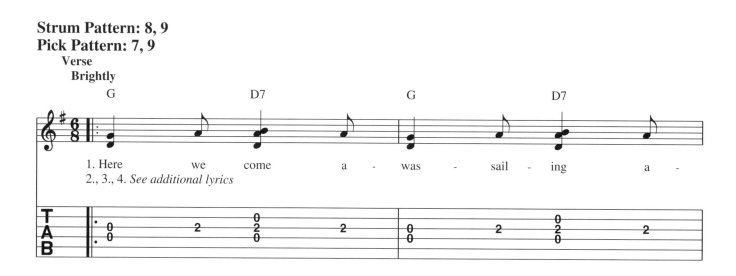

1. Here we come a-was-sail-ing a-
2., 3., 4. *See additional lyrics*

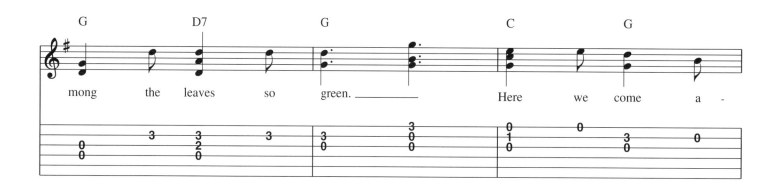

mong the leaves so green. _____ Here we come a-

Strum Pattern: 3
Pick Pattern: 3

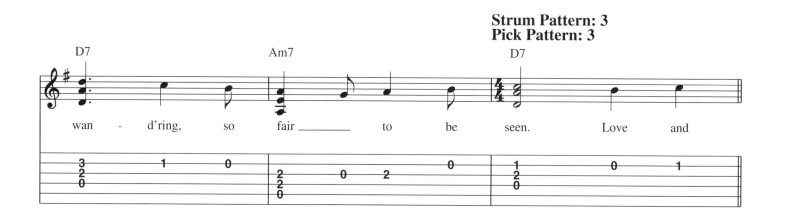

wan - d'ring, so fair _____ to be seen. Love and

Chorus

joy come to you, and to you your was - sail

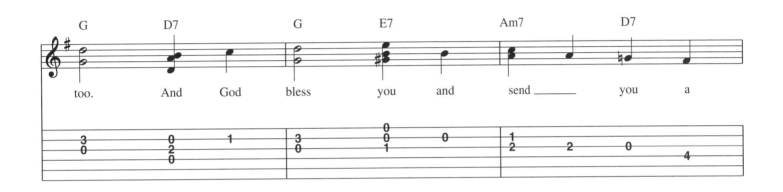

too. And God bless you and send _____ you a

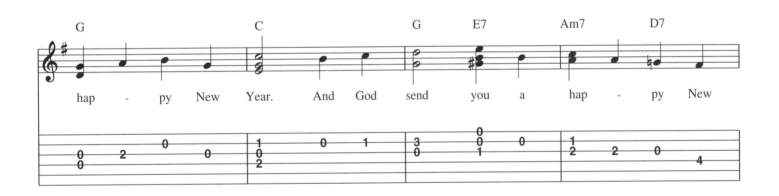

hap - py New Year. And God send you a hap - py New

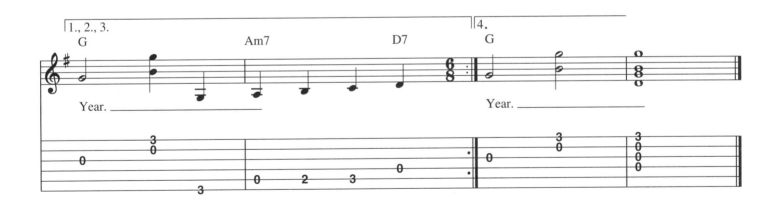

Year. _____ Year. _____

Additional Lyrics

2. We are not daily beggars
   That beg from door to door.
   But we are neighbor children
   Whom you have seen before.

3. We have got a little purse
   Of stretching leather skin.
   We want a little money
   To line it well within:

4. God bless the master of this house,
   Likewise the mistress too;
   And all the little children
   That round the table go:

A Holly Jolly Christmas

Music and Lyrics by Johnny Marks

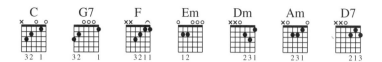

Strum Pattern: 2, 3
Pick Pattern: 3, 4

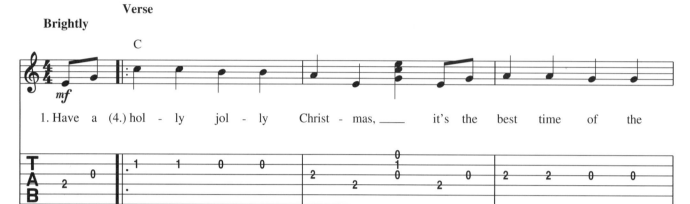

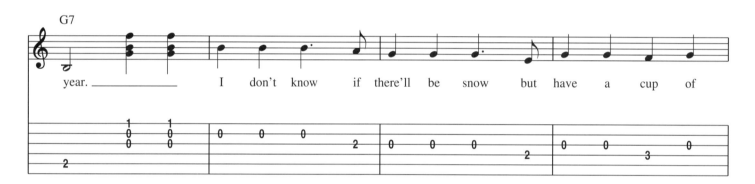

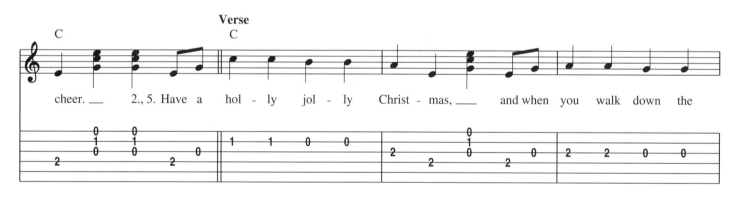

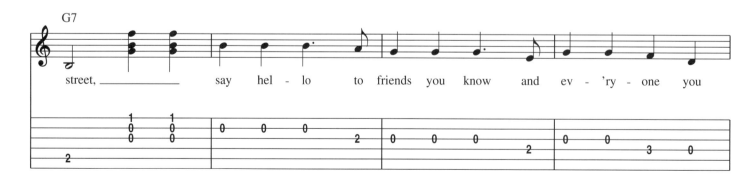

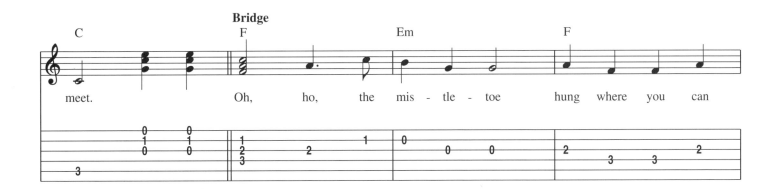

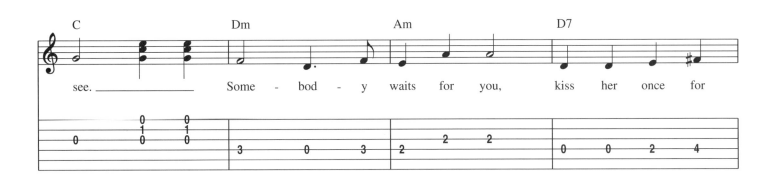

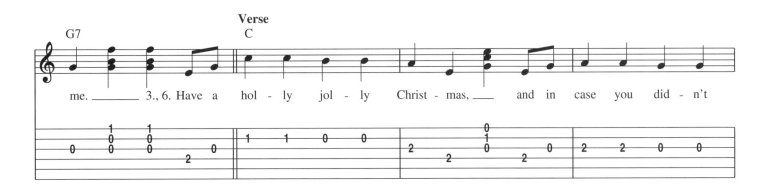

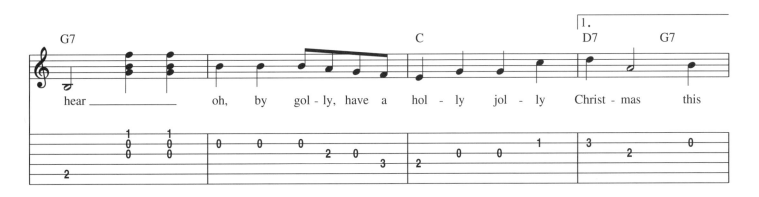

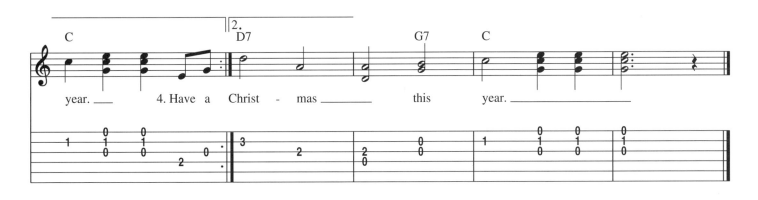

I Saw Mommy Kissing Santa Claus

Words and Music by Tommie Connor

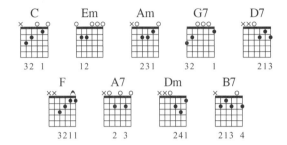

Strum Pattern: 2, 3
Pick Pattern: 3, 4

Verse
Moderately

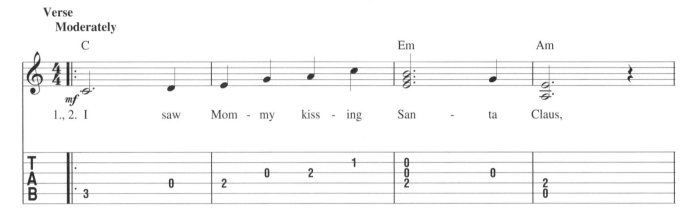

1., 2. I saw Mom - my kiss - ing San - ta Claus,

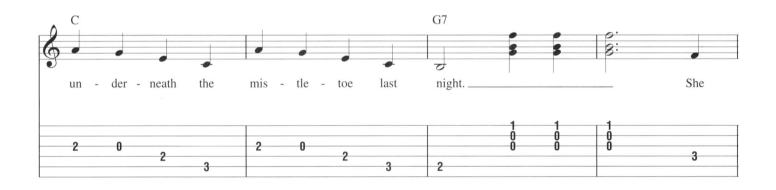

un - der - neath the mis - tle - toe last night. _____ She

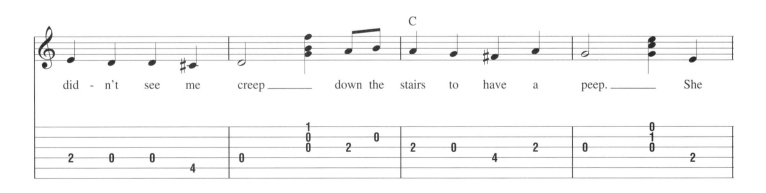

did - n't see me creep _____ down the stairs to have a peep. _____ She

thought that I was tucked up in my bed - room fast a - sleep. _____ Then

I saw Mom - my tick - le San - ta Claus, un - der - neath his

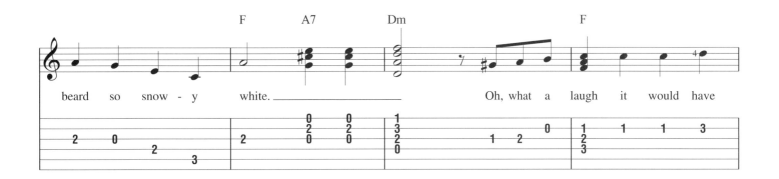

beard so snow - y white. _____ Oh, what a laugh it would have

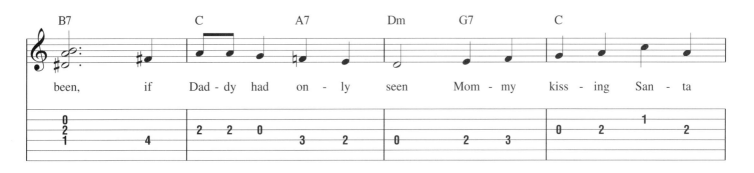

been, if Dad - dy had on - ly seen Mom - my kiss - ing San - ta

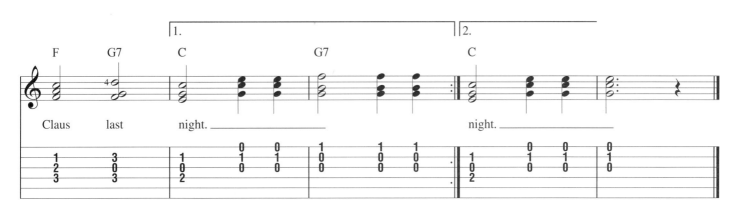

Claus last night. _____ night. _____

I'll Be Home for Christmas

Words and Music by Kim Gannon and Walter Kent

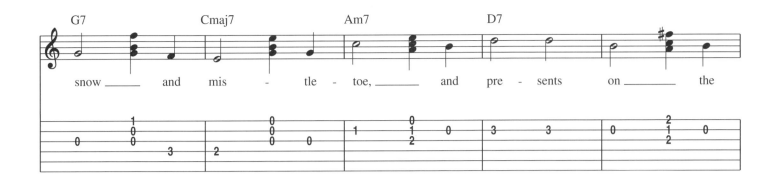

snow _____ and mis - tle - toe, _____ and pre - sents on _____ the

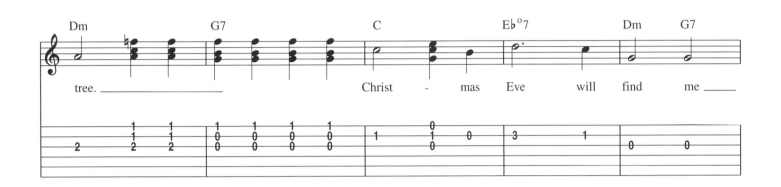

tree. _____ Christ - mas Eve will find me _____

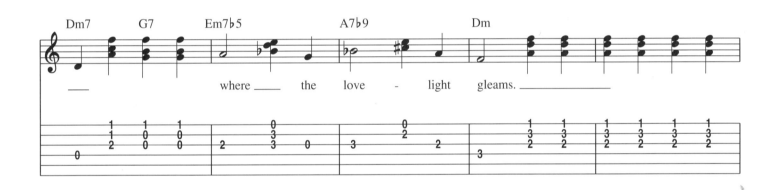

_____ where _____ the love - light gleams. _____

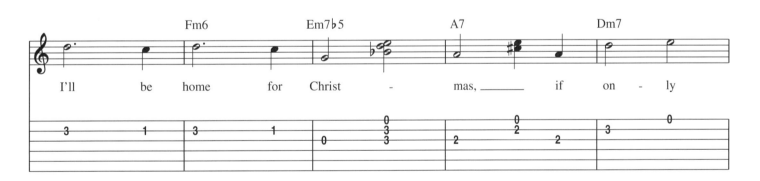

I'll be home for Christ - mas, _____ if on - ly

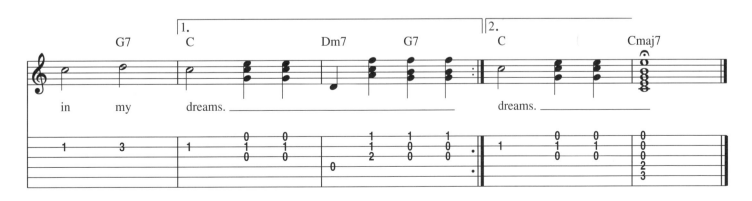

in my dreams. _____ dreams. _____

Merry Christmas, Darling

Words and Music by Richard Carpenter and Frank Pooler

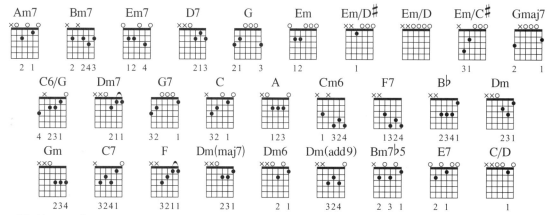

Strum Pattern: 4
Pick Pattern: 4

Intro
Freely

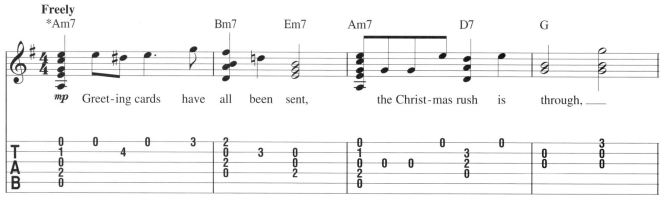

Greet-ing cards have all been sent, the Christ-mas rush is through, ___

*Let chords ring throughout Intro

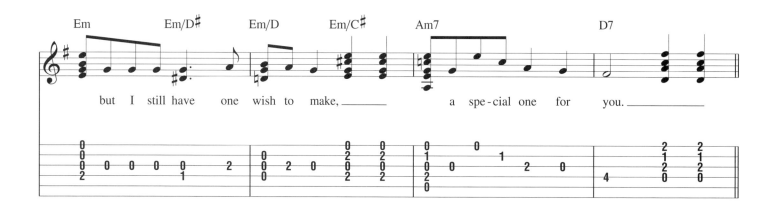

but I still have one wish to make, ___ a spe-cial one for you. ___

Verse
Moderately slow

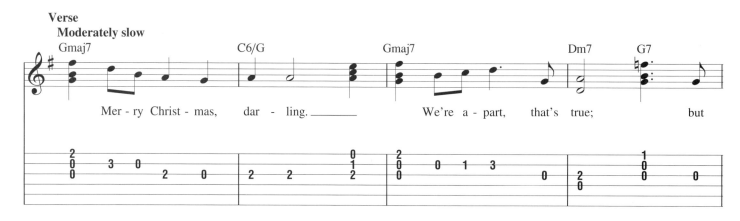

Mer-ry Christ-mas, dar-ling. ___ We're a-part, that's true; but

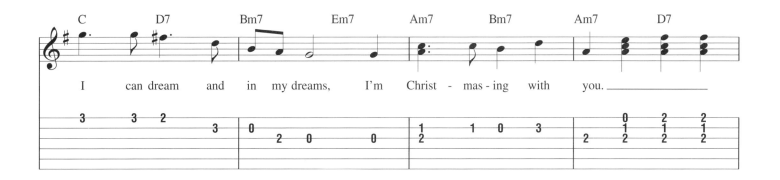

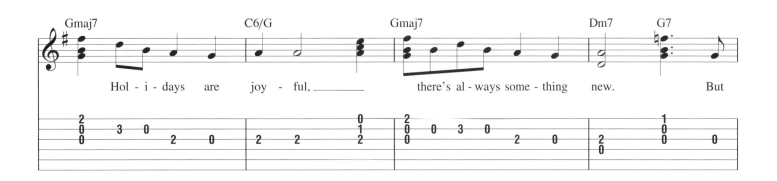

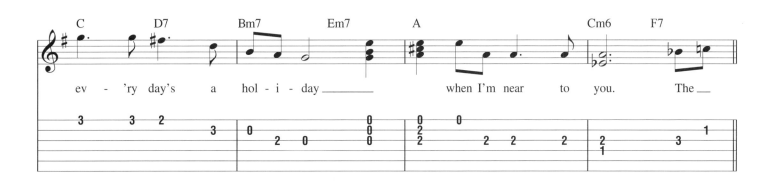

𝄋 Bridge

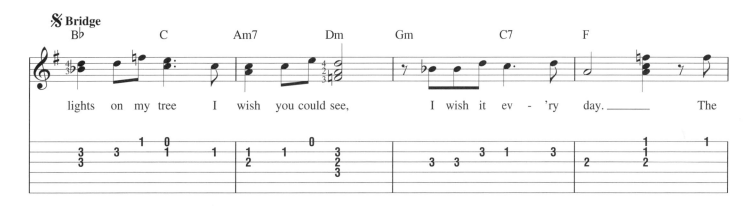

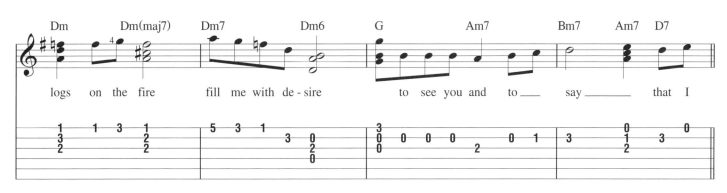

Outro-Verse

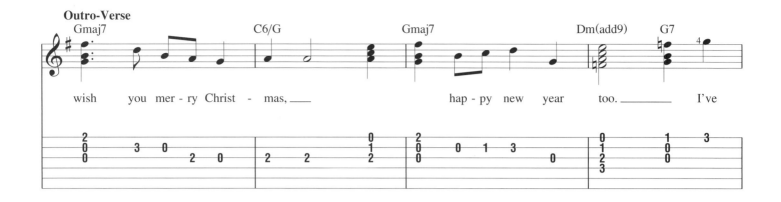

wish you mer - ry Christ - mas, ___ hap - py new year too. ___ I've

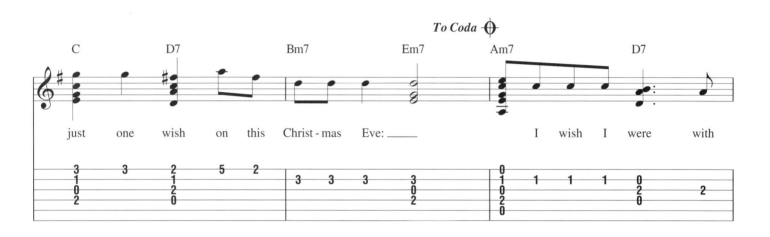

To Coda ⊕

just one wish on this Christ - mas Eve: ___ I wish I were with

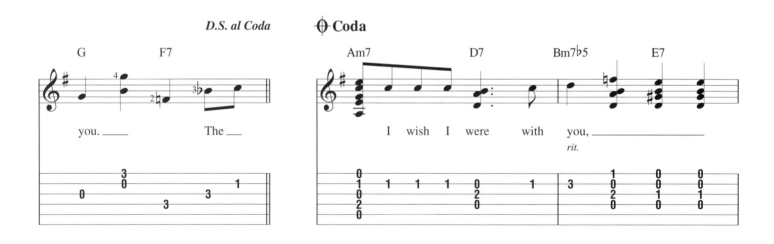

D.S. al Coda   ⊕ **Coda**

you. ___ The ___   I wish I were with you, ___ *rit.*

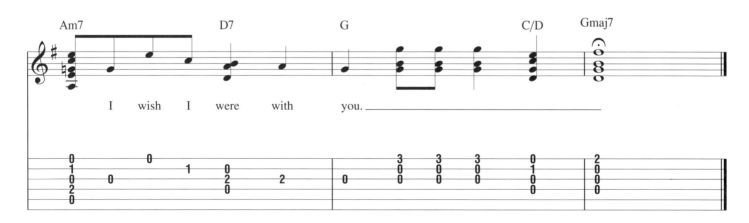

I wish I were with you. ___

The Most Wonderful Time of the Year

Words and Music by Eddie Pola and George Wyle

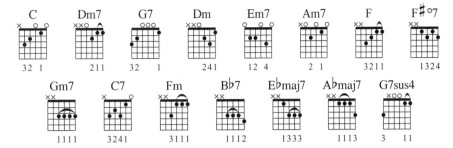

Strum Pattern: 7
Pick Pattern: 8

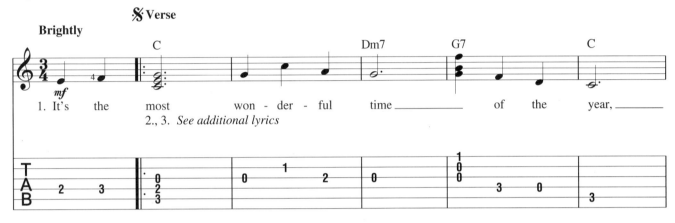

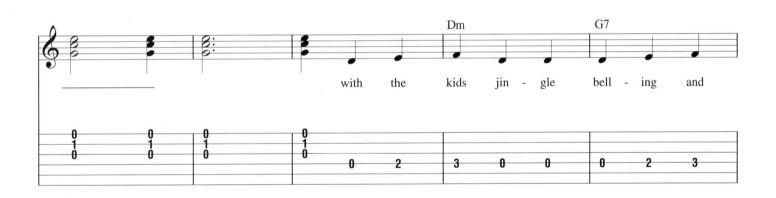

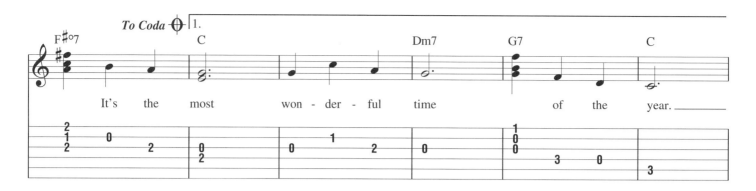

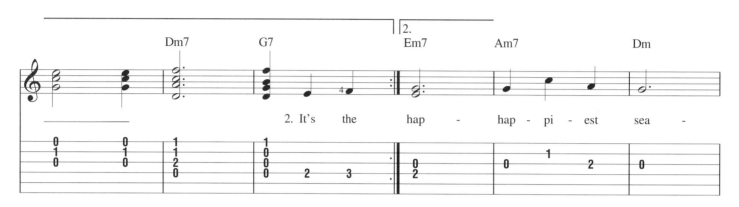

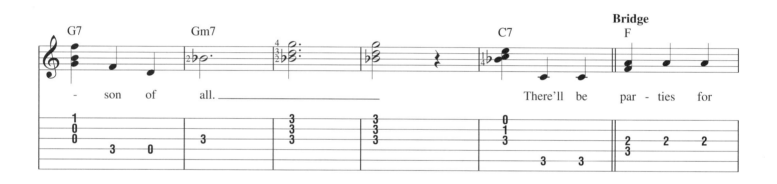

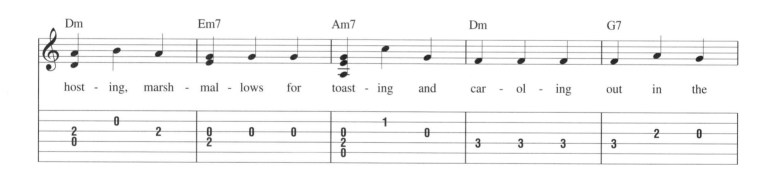

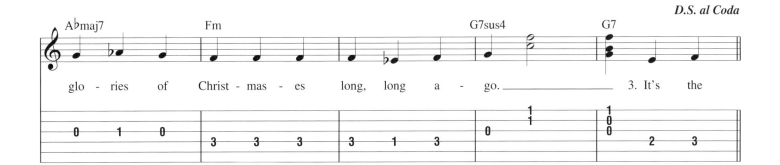

glo - ries   of   Christ - mas - es   long,   long   a - go._____   3. It's   the

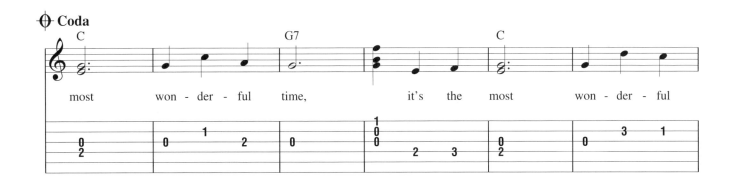

most   won - der - ful   time,   it's   the   most   won - der - ful

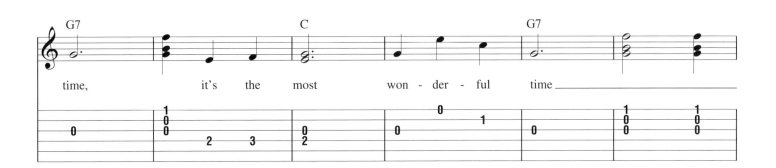

time,   it's   the   most   won - der - ful   time _____

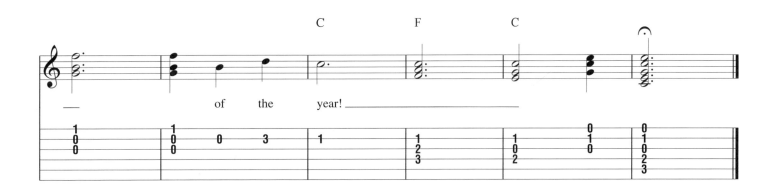

___   of   the   year! _____

Additional Lyrics

2. It's the hap-happiest season of all,
   With those holiday greetings
   And gay happy meetings
   When friends come to call.
   It's the hap-piest season of all.

3. It's the most wonderful time of the year.
   There'll be much mistletoeing
   And hearts will be glowing
   When loved ones are near.
   It's the most wonderful time,
   It's the most wonderful time,
   It's the most wonderful time of the year!

O Come, All Ye Faithful

(Adeste Fideles)

Music by John Francis Wade
Latin Words translated by Frederick Oakeley

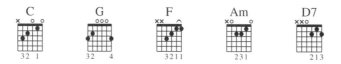

Strum Pattern: 4
Pick Pattern: 5

Verse
Triumphantly

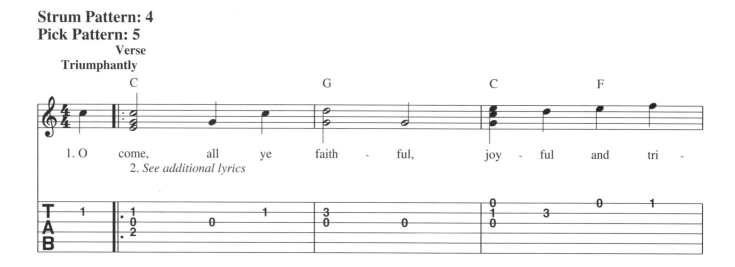

1. O come, all ye faith - ful, joy - ful and tri -
2. *See additional lyrics*

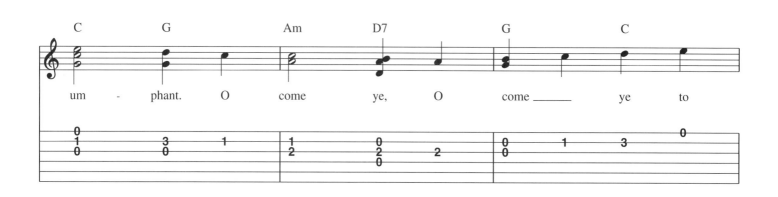

um - phant. O come ye, O come _____ ye to

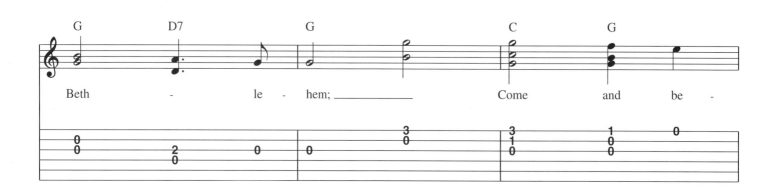

Beth - le - hem; _____ Come and be -

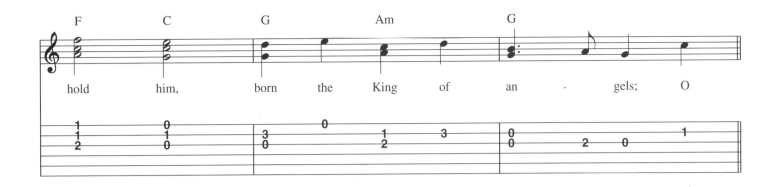

hold him, born the King of an - gels; O

Chorus

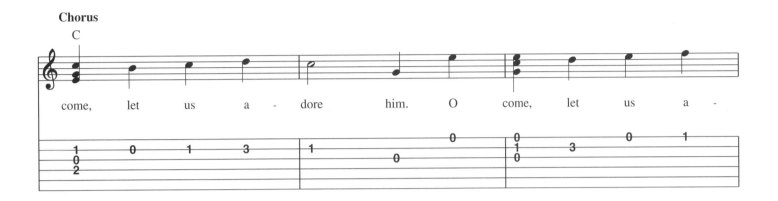

come, let us a - dore him. O come, let us a -

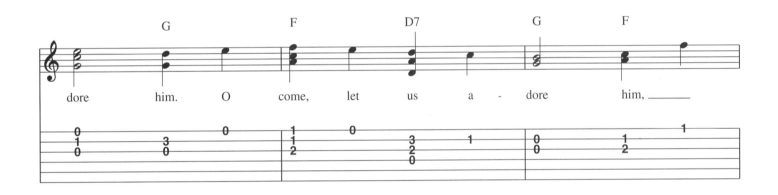

dore him. O come, let us a - dore him, _____

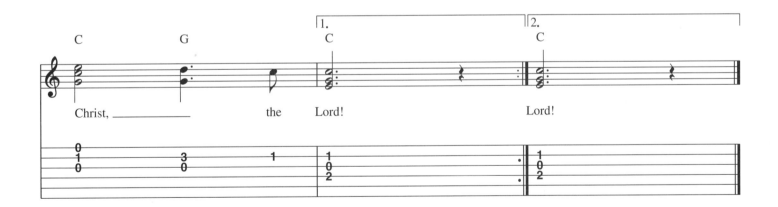

Christ, _____ the Lord! Lord!

Additional Lyrics

2. Sing choirs of angels, sing in exultation.
   O sing all ye citizens of heaven above.
   Glory to God in the highest.

O Holy Night

French Words by Placide Cappeau
English Words by John S. Dwight
Music by Adolphe Adam

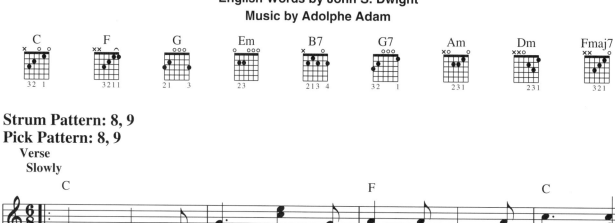

Strum Pattern: 8, 9
Pick Pattern: 8, 9

Verse
Slowly

1. O ho - ly night _____ the stars are bright - ly shin -
2. Tru - ly He taught us to love _____ one an - oth -

ing, it is the night of the dear Sav - ior's birth. _____
er. His law is love, and His gos - pel is peace. _____

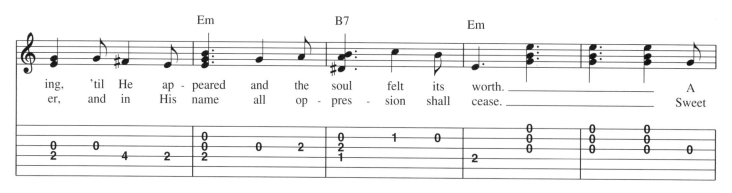

Long lay the world _____ in sin and er - ror pin -
Chains shall He break, for the slave _____ is our broth -

ing, 'til He ap - peared and the soul felt its worth. _____ A
er, and in His name all op - pres - sion shall cease. _____ Sweet

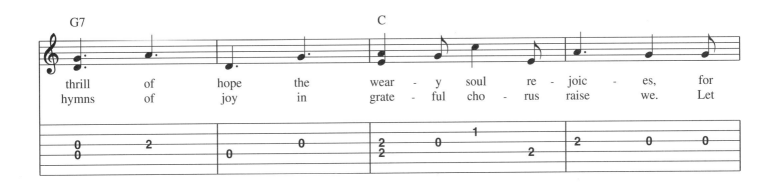

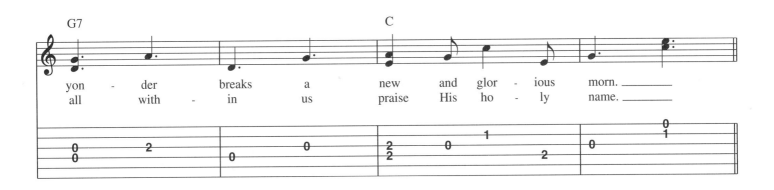

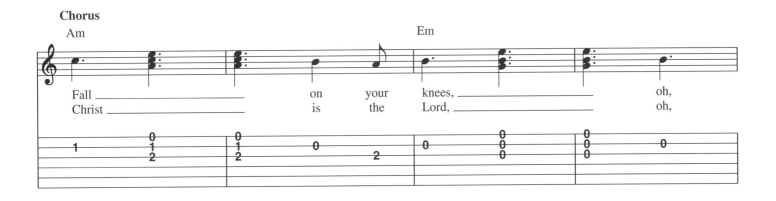

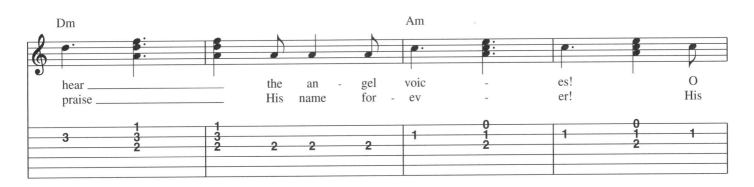

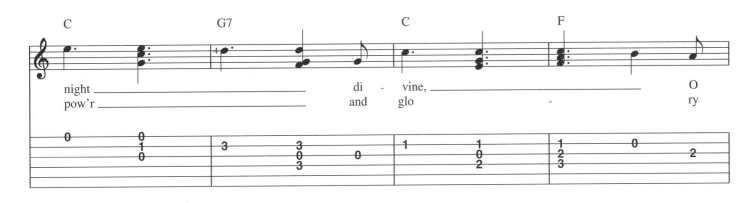

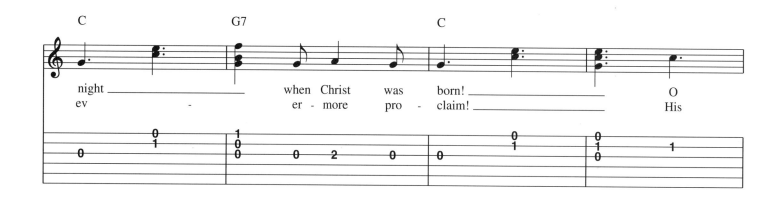

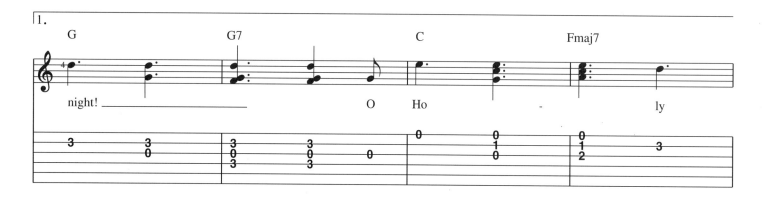

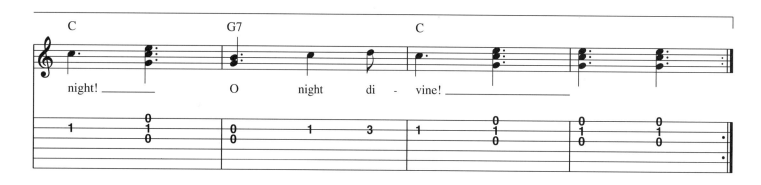

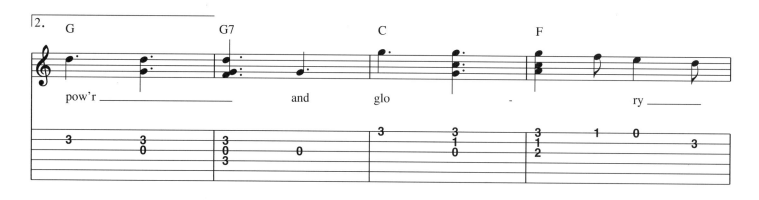

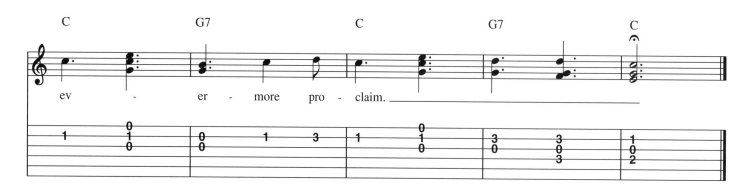

Santa Baby

By Joan Javits, Phil Springer and Tony Springer

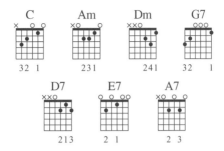

Strum Pattern: 1, 3
Pick Pattern: 2, 3

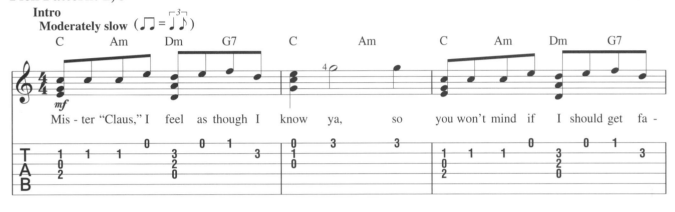

Intro
Moderately slow

Mis - ter "Claus," I feel as though I know ya, so you won't mind if I should get fa -

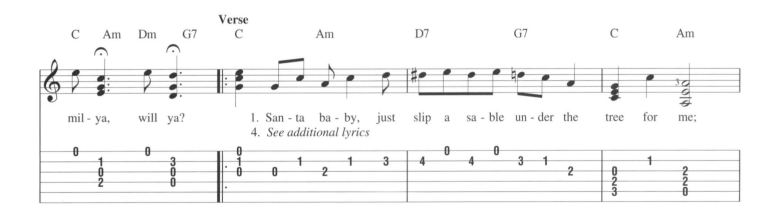

mil - ya, will ya? 1. San - ta ba - by, just slip a sa - ble un - der the tree for me;
4. *See additional lyrics*

been an aw - ful good girl. San - ta ba - by, so hur - ry down the chim - ney to -

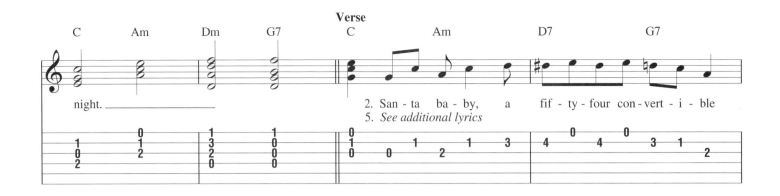

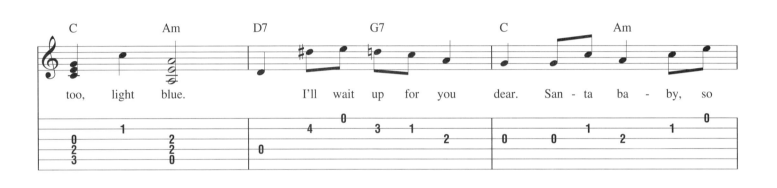

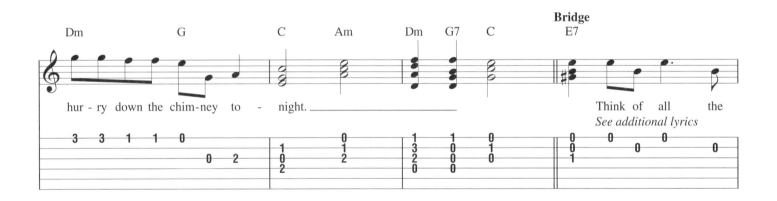

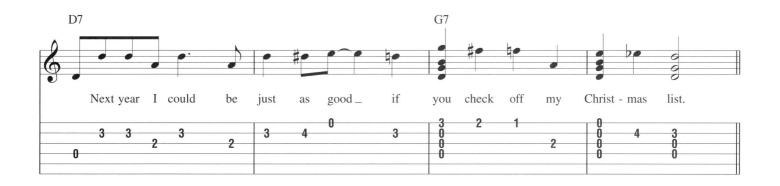

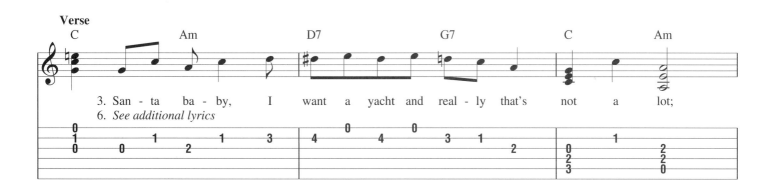

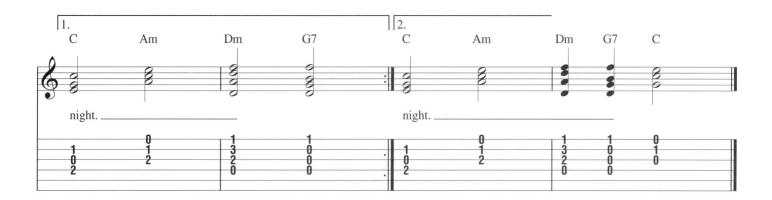

Additional Lyrics

4. Santa baby, one little thing I really do need;
   The deed to a platinum mine,
   Santa honey, so hurry down the chimney tonight.

5. Santa cutie, and fill my stockings with a duplex and cheques.
   Sign your X on the line.
   Santa cutie, and hurry down the chimney tonight.

Bridge Come and trim my Christmas tree
   With some decorations at Tiffany.
   I really do believe in you.
   Let's see if you believe in me.

6. Santa baby, forgot to mention one little thing, a ring!
   I don't mean on the phone.
   Santa baby, so hurry down the chimney tonight.

Silent Night

Words by Joseph Mohr
Translated by John F. Young
Music by Franz X. Gruber

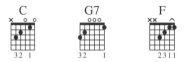

Strum Pattern: 7
Pick Pattern: 9

Verse
Quietly

1. Si - lent night, _____ ho - ly night! _____
2., 3. *See additional lyrics*

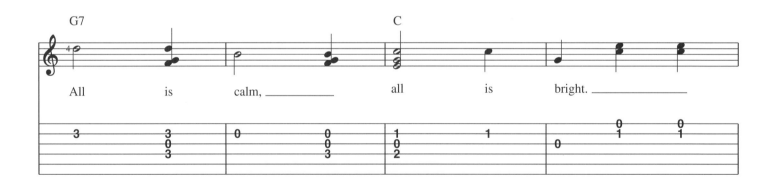

All is calm, _____ all is bright. _____

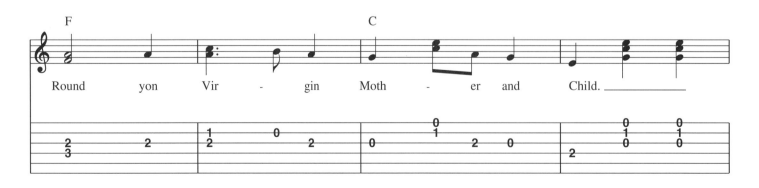

Round yon Vir - gin Moth - er and Child. _____

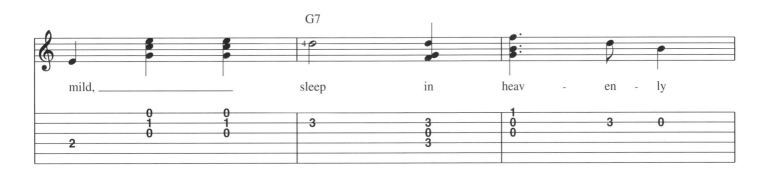

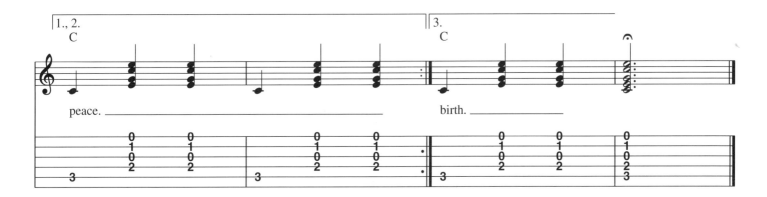

Additional Lyrics

2. Silent night, holy night!
   Shepherds quake at the sight.
   Glories stream from heaven afar.
   Heavenly hosts sing Alleluia.
   Christ the Savior is born!
   Christ the Savior is born!

3. Silent night, holy night!
   Son of God, love's pure light.
   Radiant beams from thy holy face
   With the dawn of redeeming grace.
   Jesus Lord at Thy birth.
   Jesus Lord at Thy birth.

Tennessee Christmas

Words and Music by Amy Grant and Gary Chapman

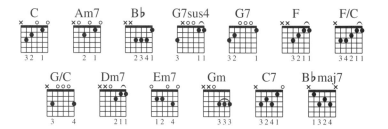

Strum Pattern: 3, 6
Pick Pattern: 3, 6

Verse
Moderately

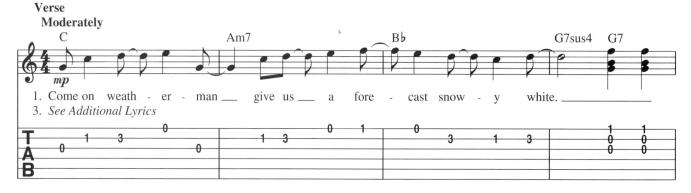

1. Come on weath-er-man __ give us __ a fore-cast snow-y white. ____
3. *See Additional Lyrics*

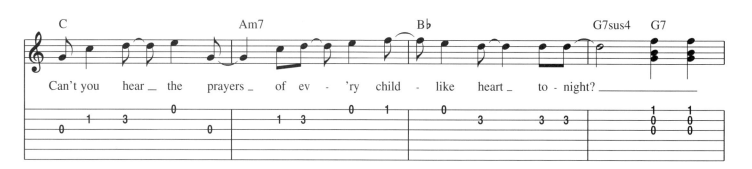

Can't you hear __ the prayers __ of ev-'ry child - like heart __ to-night? ____

Rock-ies are call - in'. Den-ver snow fall - in'. Some-bod-y said __ it's four __ feet __ deep. __ But

it does-n't mat - ter, give me the laugh - ter. I'm gon-na choose __ to __ keep __ an - oth - er

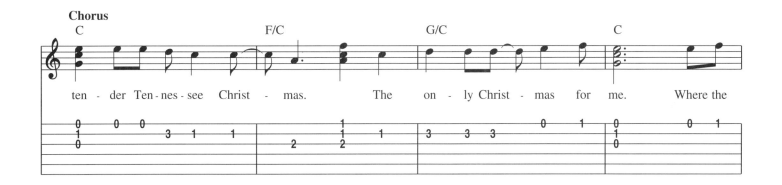

Chorus

ten - der Ten - nes - see Christ - mas. The on - ly Christ - mas for me. Where the

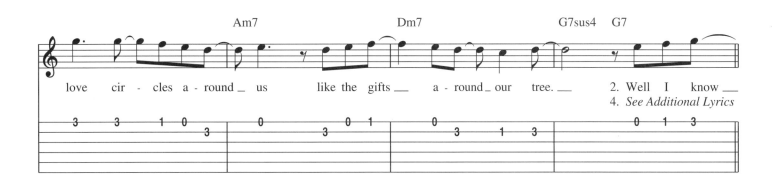

love cir - cles a - round __ us like the gifts __ a - round __ our tree. __ 2. Well I know __

4. *See Additional Lyrics*

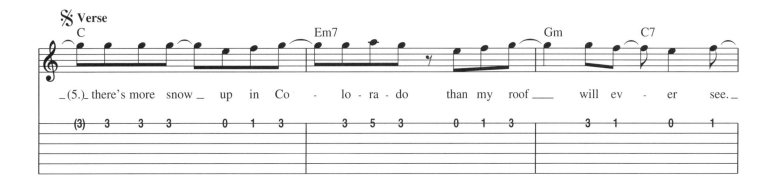

Verse

_(5.)_ there's more snow __ up in Co - lo - ra - do than my roof ___ will ev - er see. __

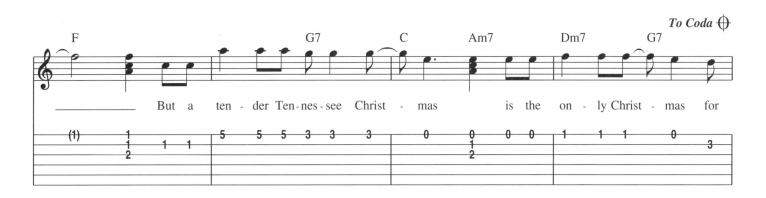

To Coda

_____ But a ten - der Ten - nes - see Christ - mas is the on - ly Christ - mas for

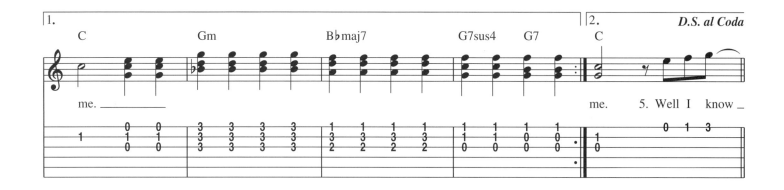

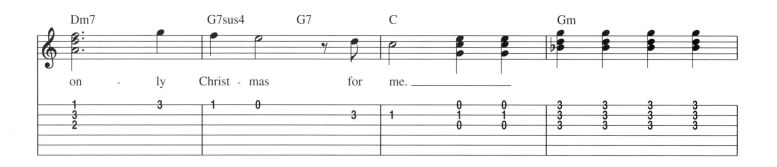

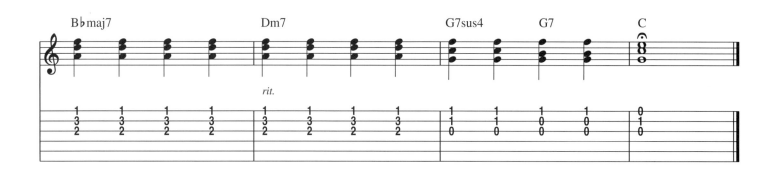

Additional Lyrics

3. Ev'ry now and then I get a wanderin' urge to see.
   Maybe California, maybe tinsel town's for me.
   There's a parade there.
   We'd have it made there.
   Bring home a tan for New Year's Eve.
   Sure sounds exciting, awfully inviting, still I think I'm gonna keep another...

4. Well they say in L.A. it's a warm holiday,
   It's the only place to be.
   But a tender Tennessee Christmas
   Is the only Christmas for me.

Angels From the Realms of Glory

Words by James Montgomery
Music by Henry T. Smart

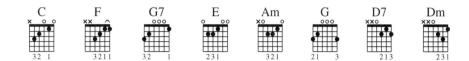

Strum Pattern: 3
Pick Pattern: 5

Verse
Joyfully

1. An - gels from the realms of glo - ry, wing your flight o'er all the earth.
2., 3., 4. *See additional lyrics*

Ye who sang cre - a - tion's sto - ry, now pro - claim Mes - si - ah's birth.

Chorus

Come and wor - ship! Come and wor - ship! Wor - ship Christ the new - born King! new - born King!

Additional Lyrics

2. Shepherds in the fields abiding,
   Watching o'er your flocks by night,
   God with men is now residing,
   Yonder shines the infant light.

3. Sages, leave your contemplations,
   Brighter visions beam afar;
   Seek the great Desire of Nations;
   Ye have seen His natal star.

4. Saints, before the altar bending,
   Watching long in hope and fear,
   Suddenly the Lord, descending,
   In His temple shall appear.

Because It's Christmas
(For All the Children)

Music by Barry Manilow
Lyric by Bruce Sussman and Jack Feldman

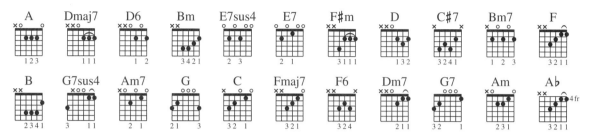

Strum Pattern: 4
Pick Pattern: 3

Verse

Moderately slow

1. To-night the stars _ shine _ for the chil - dren and light the way for dreams to
2. *See additional lyrics*

fly. To-night our love comes wrapped in _____ rib - bons.

The world is right and hopes are high. And from a dark _ and frost - ed

win - dow a child _ ap - pears to search _ the sky be - cause _ it's

Christ-mas, be-cause it's Christ-mas. Christ-mas for now _ and for - ev - er for all _ of the

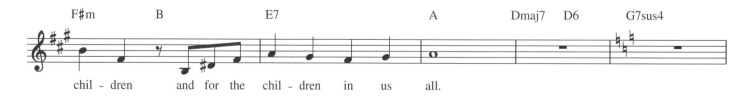

chil - dren and for the chil - dren in us all.

Additional Lyrics

2. Tonight belongs to all the children.
   Tonight their joy rings through the air.
   And so, we send our tender blessings
   To all the children ev'rywhere
   To see the smiles and hear the laughter,
   A time to give, a time to share
   Because it's Christmas for now and forever
   For all of the children in us all.

The Chipmunk Song

Words and Music by Ross Bagdasarian

Strum Pattern: 8
Pick Pattern: 8

Happily

Christ - mas, Christ - mas time is near. Time for toys and

time for cheer. We've been good but we can't last.

Hur - ry Christ - mas, hur - ry fast! Want a plane that

loops the loop. Me, I want a hu - la hoop. We can

hard - ly stand the wait. Please Christ - mas, don't be late.

The Christmas Shoes

Words and Music by Leonard Ahlstrom and Eddie Carswell

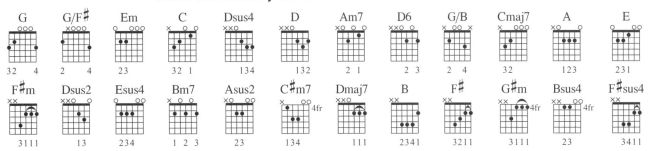

Strum Pattern: 3
Pick Pattern: 3

Verse
Moderately

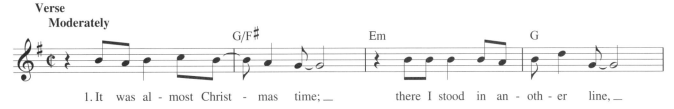

1. It was al - most Christ - mas time; __ there I stood in an - oth - er line, __

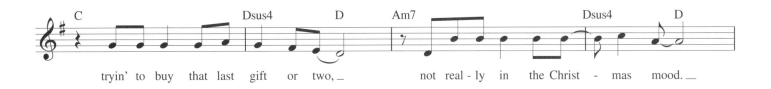

tryin' to buy that last gift or two, __ not real - ly in the Christ - mas mood. __

Stand - in' right in front __ of me was a lit - tle boy wait - ing anx - ious - ly,

pac - in' 'round like lit - tle boys do, __ and in his hands he held __ a pair of

shoes. And his clothes were worn and old, __ he was

dirt - y from head to toe. ___ But when it came ___ his time ___ to pay, ___ I

could - n't be - lieve ___ what I heard him say. "Sir, I wan - na buy these shoes ___

Chorus

___ for my ma - ma, please. ___ It's Christ - mas Eve ___ and these

shoes are just her ___ size. Could you hur - ry, sir? ___

Dad - dy says there's not much time. ___ You see, she's been sick for quite ___

___ a while ___ and I know these shoes will make ___ her smile ___ and I

want her to look beau - ti - ful ___ if Ma - ma ___ meets Je - sus ___ to -

Verse

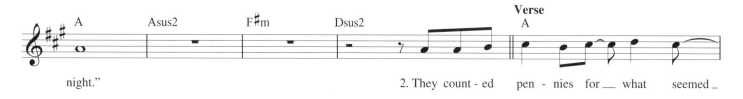

night." 2. They count - ed pen - nies for ___ what seemed ___

like years, ___ then the cash - ier said, "Son, there's not e - nough here." ___

He searched his pock - ets fran - ti - c'lly, ___ then he turned and he

looked at me. ___ He said, "Ma - ma made Christ - mas good at our house, ___ though

most years she just did with - out. ___ Tell me, sir, what am I gon - na do? ___ Some

how I've got - ta buy ___ her these Christ - mas shoes." So, I

laid the mon - ey down. ___ I just had to help ___ him out. ___ And I'll

nev - er for - get ___ the look on his face when he said, "Ma - ma's gon - na look so ___ great." ___

Chorus

___ "Sir, I wan - na buy these shoes ___ for my ma - ma, ___ please. ___

It's Christ-mas Eve __ and these shoes are just her __ size.

Could you hur - ry, sir? __ Dad - dy says there's not much time. __

__ You see, she's been sick for quite __ a while __ and I

know these shoes will make __ her smile __ and I want her to look beau -

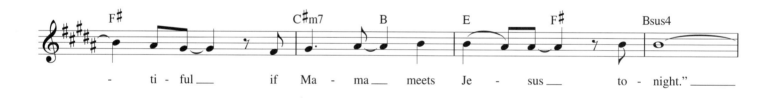

- ti - ful __ if Ma - ma __ meets Je - sus __ to - night." _____

Bridge

_____ I knew I caught a glimpse __ of heav - en's love _____ as he

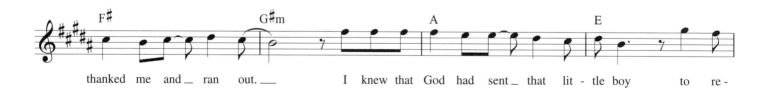

thanked me and __ ran out. __ I knew that God had sent __ that lit - tle boy to re -

mind me _____ what Christ-mas is all a - bout. *Children:* "Sir, I wan - na

Chorus

buy these shoes _____ for my ma - ma, please. _____ It's

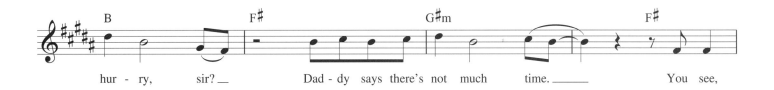

Christ - mas Eve _ and these shoes are just _ her _ size. *Add lead vocal:* Could you

hur - ry, sir? _ Dad - dy says there's not much time. _____ You see,

she's been sick for quite _ a while _ and I know these shoes will make _

_ her smile _ and I want her to look beau - ti - ful _ if

Ma - ma _ meets Je - sus _ to - night. *Boy:* I

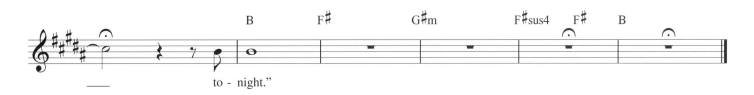

want her to _ look beau - ti - ful if Ma - ma _ meets Je - sus _

_ to - night."

Come, Thou Long-Expected Jesus

Words by Charles Wesley
Music by Rowland Hugh Prichard

Strum Pattern: 8, 7
Pick Pattern: 8, 7

Verse
Moderately

Additional Lyrics

2. Born thy people to deliver,
   Born a child and yet a king.
   Born to reign in us forever,
   Now thy gracious kingdom bring.
   By thine own eternal Spirit,
   Rule in all our hearts alone.
   By thine all-sufficient merit,
   Raise us to thy glorious throne.

Ding Dong! Merrily on High!

French Carol

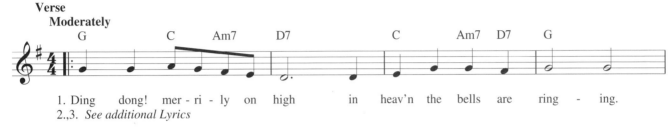

Strum Pattern: 4
Pick Pattern: 4

Verse
Moderately

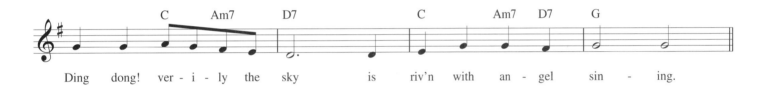

1. Ding   dong!   mer - ri - ly   on   high   in   heav'n   the   bells   are   ring   -   ing.
2.,3. *See additional Lyrics*

Ding   dong!   ver - i - ly   the   sky   is   riv'n   with   an - gel   sin   -   ing.

Chorus

Glo   -   ri - a,   Ho - san - na   in   ex - cel - sis!   cel - cis!

Additional Lyrics

2. E'en so here below, below, let steeple bells be swinging,
   And i-o, i-o, i-o, by priest and people singing.

3. Pray you, dutifully prime your matin chime, ye ringers;
   May you beautiful rime your evetime song, ye singers.

The Friendly Beasts

Traditional English Carol

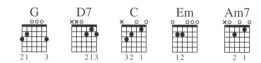

Strum Pattern: 7, 8
Pick Pattern: 8, 9

Verse

Moderately

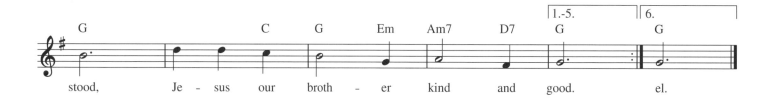

1. Je - sus our broth - er, kind and good, was hum - bly
2.-6. *See additional lyrics*

born in a sta - ble rude; and the friend - ly beasts a - round Him

stood, Je - sus our broth - er kind and good. el.

Additional Lyrics

2. "I," said the donkey, shaggy and brown,
   "I carried his mother up hill and down.
    I carried his mother to Bethlehem town."
   "I," said the donkey, shaggy and brown.

3. "I," said the cow, all white and red,
   "I gave Him my manger for His bed.
    I gave Him my hay to pillow His head."
   "I," said the cow, all white and red.

4. "I," said the sheep with the curly horn,
   "I gave Him my wool for His blanket warm.
    He wore my coat on Christmas morn."
   "I," said the sheep with the curly horn.

5. "I," said the dove from the rafters high,
   "I cooed Him to sleep that He would not cry.
    We cooed Him to sleep, my mate and I."
   "I," said the dove from the rafters high.

6. Thus every beast by some good spell,
   In the stable dark was glad to tell
   Of the gift he gave Emmanuel,
   The gift he gave Emmanuel.

Frosty the Snow Man

Words and Music by Steve Nelson and Jack Rollins

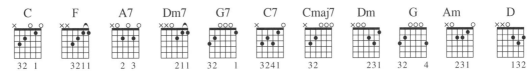

Strum Pattern: 3, 2
Pick Pattern: 3, 4

Verse
Moderately fast

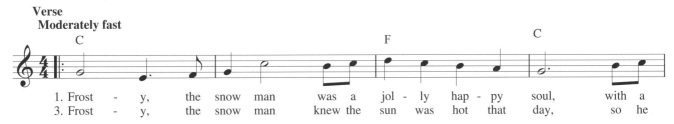

1. Frost - y, the snow man was a jol - ly hap - py soul, with a
3. Frost - y, the snow man knew the sun was hot that day, so he

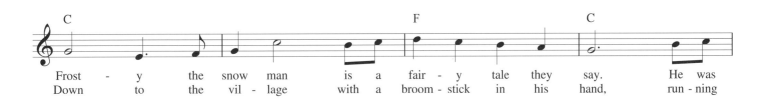

corn cob pipe and a but - ton nose and two eyes made out of coal.
said, "Let's run and we'll have some fun now be - fore I melt a - way."

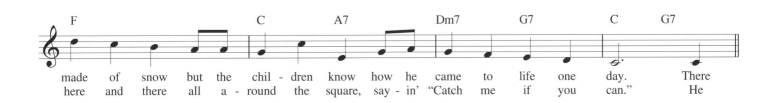

Frost - y the snow man is a fair - y tale they say. He was
Down to the vil - lage with a broom - stick in his hand, run - ning

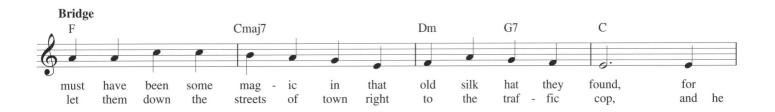

made of snow but the chil - dren know how he came to life one day. There
here and there all a - round the square, say - in' "Catch me if you can." He

Bridge

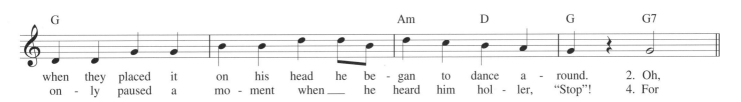

must have been some mag - ic in that old silk hat they found, for
let them down the streets of town right to the traf - ic cop, and he

when they placed it on his head he be - gan to dance a - round. 2. Oh,
on - ly paused a mo - ment when ___ he heard him hol - er, "Stop"! 4. For

Verse

Frost - y the snow man was a - live as he could be, and the
Frost - y the snow man had to hur - ry on his way, but he

chil - dren say he could laugh and play just the same as you and me.
waved good - bye say - in', "Don't you cry, I'll be back a - gain some day."

Outro

Thump - et - y thump thump, thump - et - y thump thump, look at Frost - y go.

Thump - et - y thump thump, thump - et - y thump thump, o - ver the hills of snow.

Here Comes Santa Claus
(Right Down Santa Claus Lane)

Words and Music by Gene Autry and Oakley Haldeman

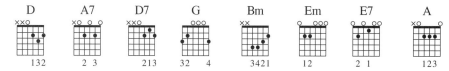

Strum Pattern: 3
Pick Pattern: 3

Intro   Verse
Moderately fast

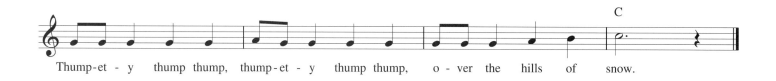

Play 4 times

1. Here comes San - ta Claus, here comes San - ta Claus
2. Here comes San - ta Claus, here comes San - ta Claus
3., 4. *See additional lyrics*

right down San - ta Claus lane.   Vix - en, Blit - zen,
right down San - ta Claus lane.   He's got a bag that's

all of his rein - deer pull - ing all ___ the reins. ___
filled ___ with toys for boys and girls a - gain. ___

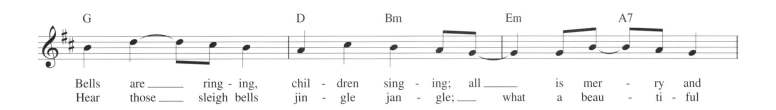

Bells are ___ ring - ing, chil - dren sing - ing; all ___ is mer - ry and
Hear those ___ sleigh bells jin - gle jan - gle; ___ what a beau - ti - ful

bright. Hang your stock - ings and say your prayers, _ 'cause San -
sight. Jump in bed and cov - er up your head, 'cause San -

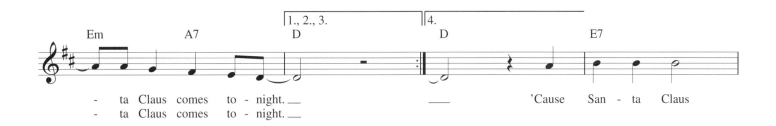

1., 2., 3.   4.

- ta Claus comes to - night. ___   'Cause San - ta Claus
- ta Claus comes to - night. ___

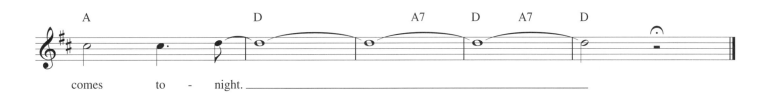

comes to - night. _____

Additional Lyrics

3. Here comes Santa Claus, here comes Santa Claus
   Right down Santa Claus lane.
   He doesn't care if you're rich or poor,
   For he loves you just the same.
   Santa knows that we're God's children;
   That makes ev'rything right.
   Fill your hearts with Christmas cheer
   'Cause Santa Claus comes tonight.

4. Here comes Santa Claus, here comes Santa Claus
   Right down Santa Claus lane.
   He'll come around when the chimes ring out;
   It's Christmas morn again.
   Peace on earth will come to all
   If we just follow the Light.
   Let's give thanks to the Lord above,
   'Cause Santa Claus comes tonight.

The Gift

Words and Music by Tom Douglas and Jim Brickman

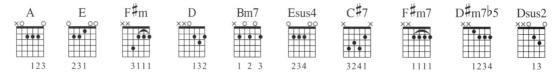

Strum Pattern: 3, 6
Pick Pattern: 4

Verse
Slowly

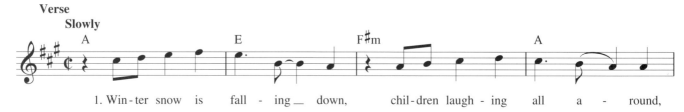

1. Win-ter snow is fall-ing down, chil-dren laugh-ing all a-round,

lights are turn-ing on, like a fair-y tale come true.

Sit-ting by the fire we made, you're the an-swer when I prayed

I would find some-one and, ba-by, I found you.

Chorus

All I want is to hold you for-ev-er. All I need

is you more ev-'ry day. You saved my heart

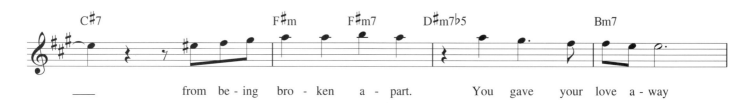

from be-ing bro-ken a-part. You gave your love a-way

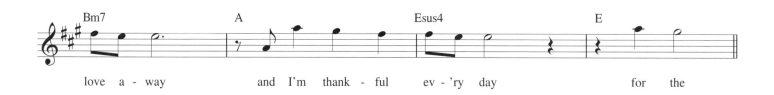

love a - way   and I'm thank - ful ev - 'ry day   for the

Interlude

gift.

D.S. al Coda

All I want

𝄌 Coda

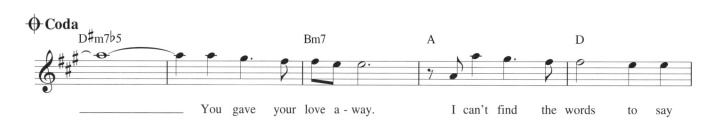

You gave your love a - way.   I can't find the words to say

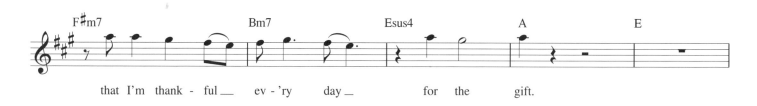

that I'm thank - ful ev - 'ry day   for the   gift.

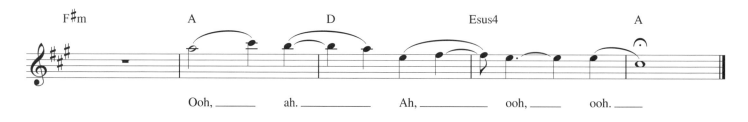

Ooh, ____ ah. ____ Ah, ____ ooh, ____ ooh. ____

Good King Wenceslas

Words by John M. Neale
Music from *Piae Cantiones*

Strum Pattern: 4, 3
Pick Pattern: 5, 3

Verse
With spirit

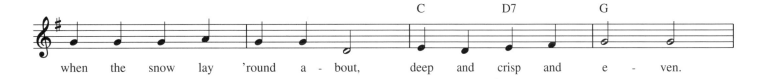

1. Good King Wen - ces - las looked out on the feast of Ste - phen;
2.-5. *See additional lyrics*

when the snow lay 'round a - bout, deep and crisp and e - ven.

Bright - ly shone the moon that night, though the frost was cru - el; when a poor man

came in sight, gath - 'ring win - ter fu - el. ing.

Additional Lyrics

2. "Hither page, and stand by me,
If thou know'st it, telling;
Yonder peasant, who is he?
Where and what his dwelling?"
"Sire, he lives a good league hence,
Underneath the mountain;
Right against the forest fence,
By Saint Agnes' fountain."

3. "Bring me flesh, and bring me wine,
Bring me pine-logs hither;
Thou and I will see him dine,
When we bear them thither."
Page and monarch forth they went,
Forth they went together;
Through the rude winds wild lament,
And the bitter weather.

4. "Sire, the night is darker now,
And the wind blows stronger;
Fails my heart, I know not how,
I can go not longer."
"Mark my footsteps, my good page,
Tread thou in them boldly:
Thou shalt find the winter's rage
Freeze thy blood less coldly."

5. In his master's steps he trod,
Where the snow lay dinted;
Heat was in the very sod
Which the saint has printed.
Therefore, Christian men, be sure,
Wealth or rank possessing;
Ye who now will bless the poor,
Shall yourselves find blessing.

The Holly and the Ivy

18th Century English Carol

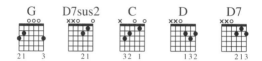

Strum Pattern: 8
Pick Pattern: 8

Verse
Moderately slow

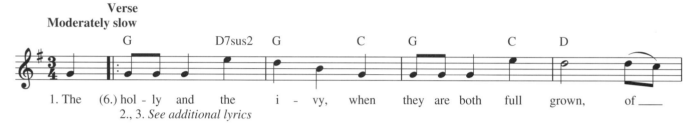

1. The (6.) hol - ly and the i - vy, when they are both full grown, of ___
2., 3. *See additional lyrics*

all the trees that are in the wood, the ___ hol - ly bears the crown. The

Chorus

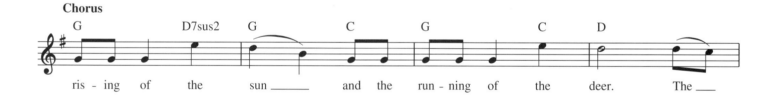

ris - ing of the sun ___ and the run - ning of the deer. The ___

play - ing of the mer - ry or - gan, sweet sing - ing of the choir. 2. The choir.

Additional Lyrics

2. The holly bears a blossom,
   As white as lily flow'r,
   And Mary bore sweet Jesus Christ,
   To be our sweet Saviour.

3. The holly bears a berry,
   As red as any blood,
   And Mary bore sweet Jesus Christ,
   To do poor sinners good.

4. The holly bears a pickle,
   As sharp as any thorn,
   And Mary bore sweet Jesus Christ
   On Christmas Day in the morn.

5. The holly bears a bark,
   As bitter as any gall,
   And Mary bore sweet Jesus Christ
   For to redeem us all.

Jingle Bells

Words and Music by J. Pierpont

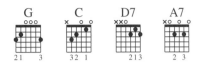

Strum Pattern: 2, 3
Pick Pattern: 3, 4

Verse
Brightly

1. Dash-ing through the snow, in a one horse o-pen sleigh. O'er the fields we go,
2., 3. *See additional lyrics*

laugh-ing all the way. Bells on bob-tail ring, mak-ing spir-its bright. What fun it is to

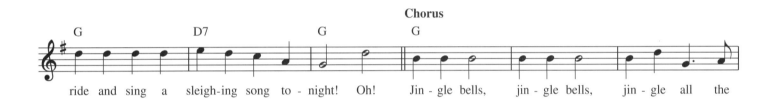

ride and sing a sleigh-ing song to-night! Oh! Jin - gle bells, jin - gle bells, jin - gle all the

way. Oh, what fun it is to ride in a one horse o-pen sleigh! __ Jin - gle bells,

jin-gle bells, jin-gle all the way. Oh, what fun it is to ride in a one horse o-pen sleigh! 2. A sleigh!

Additional Lyrics

2. A day or two ago, I thought I'd take a ride,
And soon Miss Fannie Bright was sitting by my side.
The horse was lean and lank,
Misfortune seemed his lot.
He got into a drifted bank and we, we got upshot! Oh!

3. Now the ground is white, go it while you're young.
Take the girls tonight and sing this sleighing song.
Just get a bobtail bay,
Two-forty for his speed.
Then hitch him to an open sleigh and
Crack, you'll take the lead! Oh!

I Heard the Bells on Christmas Day

Words by Henry Wadsworth Longfellow
Music by John Baptiste Calkin

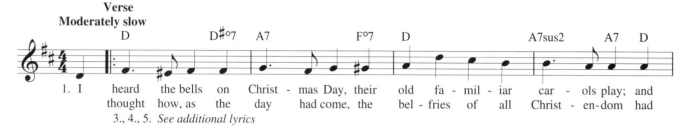

Strum Pattern: 4
Pick Pattern: 3

Verse
Moderately slow

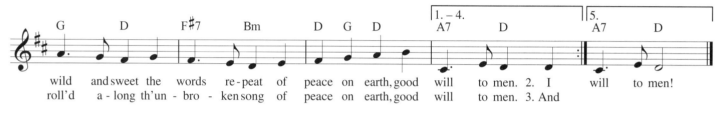

1. I heard the bells on Christ-mas Day, their old fa-mil-iar car-ols play; and
thought how, as the day had come, the bel-fries of all Christ-en-dom had

3., 4., 5. *See additional lyrics*

wild and sweet the words re-peat of peace on earth, good will to men. 2. I will to men!
roll'd a-long th'un-bro-ken song of peace on earth, good will to men. 3. And

Additional Lyrics

3. And in despair I bow'd my head:
"There is no peace on earth," I said.
"For hate is strong, and mocks the song
Of peace on earth, good will to men."

4. Then pealed the bells more loud and deep:
"God is not dead, nor doth He sleep;
The wrong shall fail, the right prevail,
With peace on earth, good will to men."

5. Till, ringing, singing on its way,
The world revolved from night to day,
A voice, a chime, a chant sublime,
Of peace on earth, good will to men!

It's Beginning to Look Like Christmas

By Meredith Willson

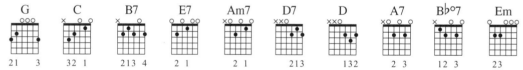

Strum Pattern: 2, 3
Pick Pattern: 3, 4

𝄋 Verse

Brightly

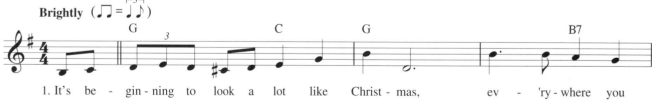

1. It's be-gin-ning to look a lot like Christ-mas, ev-'ry-where you

go.   { Take a look in the five and ten, glis-ten-ing once a-gain with
         { There's a tree in the grand ho-tel, one in the park, as well; the

can - dy canes and sil - ver lanes a - glow. ⎫ It's be - gin - ning to look a lot like Christ - mas,
stur - dy kind that does - n't mind the snow. ⎭

toys in ev - 'ry store. ⎫ But the pret - ti - est sight to see is the
soon the bells will start. ⎭ And the thing that will make them ring is the

To Coda ⊕

hol - ly that will be, on your own front door A pair of
car - ol that you sing right with - in your

Bridge

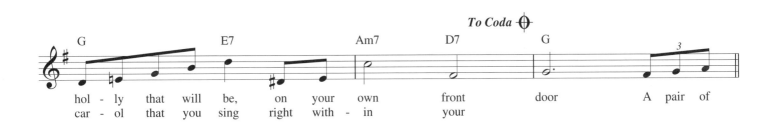

hop - a - long boots and a pis - tol that shoots is the wish of Bar - ney and Ben.

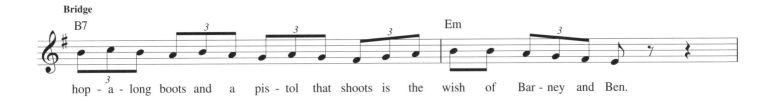

Dolls that will talk and will go for a walk is the hope of Jan - ice and Jen. And

⊕ **Coda**

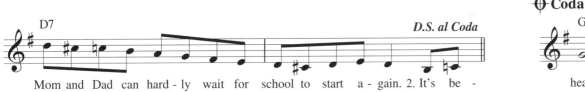

D.S. al Coda

Mom and Dad can hard - ly wait for school to start a - gain. 2. It's be -   heart.

I've Got My Love to Keep Me Warm

from the 20th Century Fox Motion Picture ON THE AVENUE
Words and Music by Irving Berlin

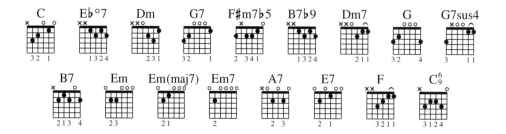

Strum Pattern: 3, 4
Pick Pattern: 3, 4

Verse

Brightly

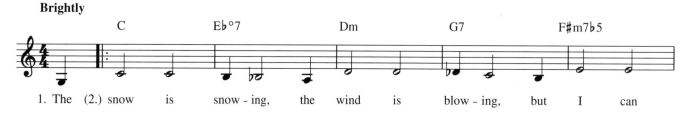

1. The (2.) snow is snow-ing, the wind is blow-ing, but I can

weath - er the storm. ___ What do I care how much it may storm?___

___ I've got my love to keep me warm.

I can't re - mem - ber a worse De - cem - ber; just

watch those i - ci - cles form. _____ What do I care if

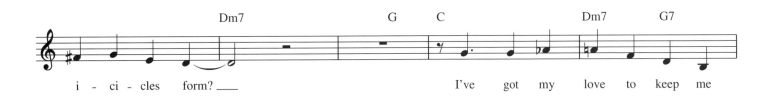

i - ci - cles form? _____ I've got my love to keep me

Bridge

warm. Off with my o - ver - coat, _ off with my

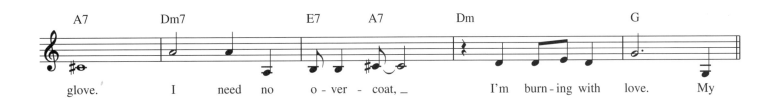

glove. I need no o - ver - coat, _ I'm burn - ing with love. My

Outro-Verse

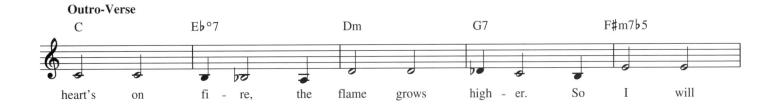

heart's on fi - re, the flame grows high - er. So I will

weath - er the storm. _____ What do I care how much it may storm? _

I've got my love to keep me warm. 2. The warm. _____

It Must Have Been the Mistletoe
(Our First Christmas)

By Justin Wilde and Doug Konecky

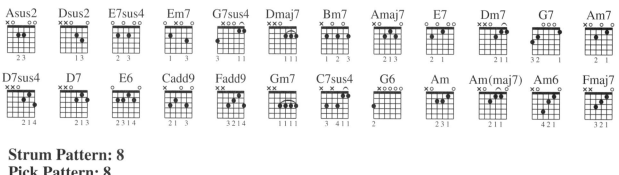

Strum Pattern: 8
Pick Pattern: 8

Verse

Moderately

1. It must have been _ the mis-tle-toe, _ the la-zy fire, _ the fall-ing snow, _ the

mag - ic in _____ the frost - y air, ___ that feel - ing ev - 'ry - where. It

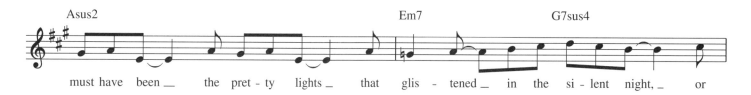

must have been _ the pret-ty lights _ that glis - tened _ in the si - lent night, _ or

may - be just ____ the stars so bright _ that shined a - bove you.

Bridge

Our first Christ - mas, more than _ we'd been dream - ing of. _

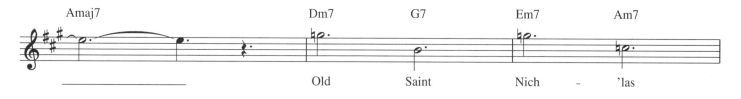

Old Saint Nich - 'las

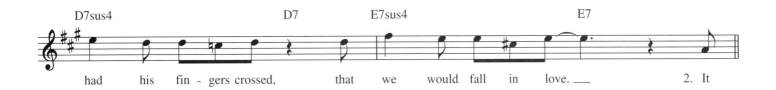

had his fin - gers crossed, that we would fall in love. ___ 2. It

Verse

could have been ___ the hol - i - day, ___ the mid - night ride ___ up - on a sleigh, ___ the

coun - try - side ___ all dressed in white, ___ that cra - zy snow - ball fight. It

could have been ___ the stee - ple bell ___ that wrapped us up with - in it's spell. ___ It

on - ly took one kiss to know, ___ it must have been the

Bridge

mis - tle - toe. Our first Christ - mas,

more than ___ we'd been dream - ing of. ___ Old Saint

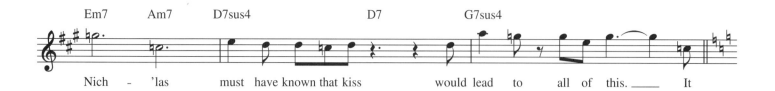

Em7   Am7   D7sus4   D7   G7sus4

Nich - 'las   must have known that kiss   would lead to   all of this. _____   It

Outro

Cadd9

must have been __   the mis - tle - toe, ___   the la - zy fire, ___   the fall - ing snow, _   the

Fadd9   G7sus4

mag - ic in _____   the frost - y air, ____   that made   me   love   you.   On

Cadd9   Gm7   C7sus4

Christ - mas Eve ___   a wish come true, __   that night I _____ fell in love with you. __   It

Fadd9   Dm7   G7sus4

on - ly took __   one kiss to know, __   it must have been   the

Cadd9   Dm7   G6   Am   Am(maj7) Am7   Am6

mis - tle - toe!   It must have been   the mis - tle - toe!   It

Dm7   G7sus4   Cadd9   Fmaj7   Cadd9

must have been   the mis - tle - toe!

Joy to the World

Words by Isaac Watts
Music by George Frideric Handel
Adapted by Lowell Mason

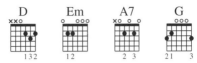

Strum Pattern: 3
Pick Pattern: 3

Verse

With spirit

1. Joy to the World! The Lord is come: Let earth re-
2., 3., 4. *See additional lyrics*

ceive her King. Let ev - 'ry ___ heart ___ pre - pare ___ Him ___

room, ___ and heav - en and na - ture ___ sing, and ___ heav - en and na - ture

sing, and ___ heav - en and heav - en and na - ture sing. love.

Additional Lyrics

2. Joy to the world! The Savior reigns;
   Let men their songs employ;
   While fields and floods,
   Rocks, hills and plains,
   Repeat the sounding joy,
   Repeat the sounding joy,
   Repeat, repeat the sounding joy.

3. No more let sin and sorrow grow,
   Nor thorns infest the ground;
   He comes to make His blessings flow
   Far as the curse is found,
   Far as the curse is found,
   Far as, far as the curse is found.

4. He rules the world with truth and grace
   And makes the nations prove
   The glories of His righteousness,
   And wonders of His love,
   And wonders of His love,
   And wonders, wonders of His love.

The Last Month of the Year
(What Month Was Jesus Born In?)

Words and Music by Vera Hall
Adapted and Arranged by Ruby Pickens Tartt and Alan Lomax

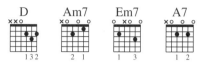

Strum Pattern: 6
Pick Pattern: 3

Verse

Moderately

1. What month was my Je-sus born in? Last month of the year!
2., 3., 4 *See additional lyrics*

What month was my Je-sus born in? Last month of the year! Oh,

Chorus

Jan-u-ar-y, Feb-ru-ar-y, March,

A-pril, May, June, O Lord, You got Ju-ly, Au-gust, Sep-tem-ber, Oc-

to-ber and a No-vem-ber, on the twen-ty fifth day of De-cem-ber in the

1., 2., 3. | **4.**

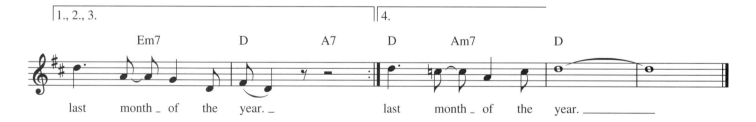

last month of the year. last month of the year.

Additional Lyrics

2. Well, they laid Him in the manger,
Last month of the year!
Well, they laid Him in the manger,
Last month of the year!

3. Wrapped Him up in swaddling clothing,
Last month of the year!
Wrapped Him up in swaddling clothing,
Last month of the year!

4. He was born of the Virgin Mary,
Last month of the year!
He was born of the Virgin Mary,
Last month of the year!

A Marshmallow World

Words by Carl Sigman
Music by Peter De Rose

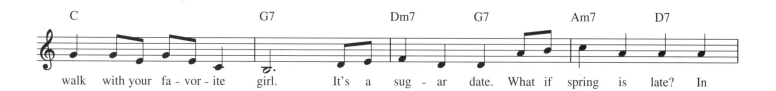

walk with your fa-vor-ite girl. It's a sug-ar date. What if spring is late? In

D.S. al Coda
(take repeat)

⊕ **Coda**

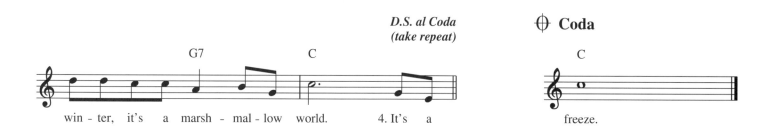

win - ter, it's a marsh - mal - low world. 4. It's a

freeze.

Nuttin' for Christmas

Words and Music by Roy Bennett and Sid Tepper

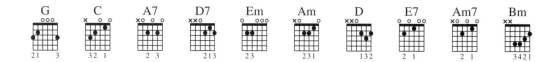

Strum Pattern: 4
Pick Pattern: 5

Verse
Brightly

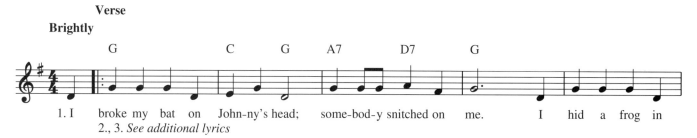

1. I broke my bat on John-ny's head; some-bod-y snitched on me. I hid a frog in
2., 3. *See additional lyrics*

sis-ter's bed; some-bod-y snitched on me. I spilled some ink on Mom-my's rug, I made Tom-my

eat a bug, bought some gum with a pen-ny slug; some-bod-y snitched on me. Oh,

Chorus

I'm get-tin' nut-tin' for Christ-mas. Mom-my and Dad-dy are

mad. I'm get-tin' nut-tin' for Christ-mas, 'cause

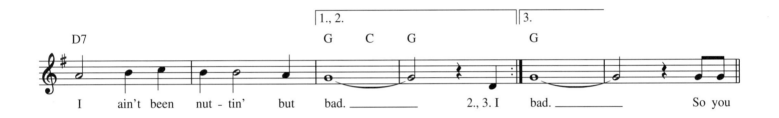

I ain't been nut-tin' but bad._____ 2., 3. I bad._____ So you

Outro

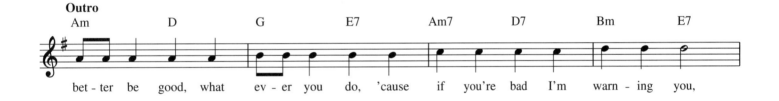

bet-ter be good, what-ev-er you do, 'cause if you're bad I'm warn-ing you,

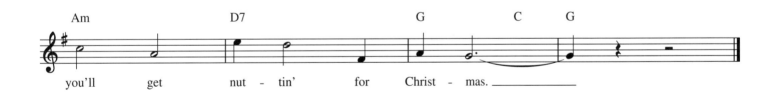

you'll get nut-tin' for Christ-mas._____

Additional Lyrics

2. I put a tack on teacher's chair;
   Somebody snitched on me.
   I tied a knot in Susie's hair;
   Somebody snitched on me.
   I did a dance on Mommy's plants,
   Climbed a tree and tore my pants.
   Filled the sugar bowl with ants;
   Somebody snitched on me.

3. I won't be seeing Santa Claus;
   Somebody snitched on me.
   He won't come visit me because
   Somebody snitched on me.
   Next year, I'll be going straight.
   Next year, I'll be good, just wait.
   I'd start now but it's too late;
   Somebody snitched on me, oh,

O Christmas Tree

Traditional German Carol

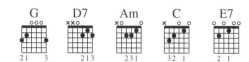

Strum Pattern: 8, 7
Pick Pattern: 8, 9

Verse
Moderately

1. O, Christ-mas tree! O, Christ-mas tree, ___ you stand in ver - dant beau - ty! O,
2., 3. *See additional lyrics*

Christ - mas tree, O, Christ-mas tree, ___ you stand in ver - dant beau - ty! Your

boughs are green ___ in sum-mer's glow, ___ and do not fade ___ in win-ter's snow. O,

Christ-mas tree, O, Christ - mas tree, ___ you stand in ver - dant beau - ty! 2. O, bright - ly.

Additional Lyrics

2. O, Christmas tree! O, Christmas tree,
Much pleasure doth thou bring me!
O, Christmas tree! O, Christmas tree,
Much pleasure does thou bring me!
For every year the Christmas tree
Brings to us all both joy and glee.
O, Christmas tree, O, Christmas tree,
Much pleasure doth thou bring me!

3. O, Christmas tree! O, Christmas tree,
Thy candles shine out brightly!
O, Christmas Tree, O, Christmas tree,
Thy candles shine out brightly!
Each bough doth hold its tiny light
That makes each toy to sparkle bright.
O, Christmas tree, O Christmas tree,
Thy candles shine out brightly.

O Come, O Come Immanuel

Plainsong, 13th Century
Words translated by John M. Neale and Henry S. Coffin

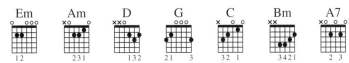

Strum Pattern: 4
Pick Pattern: 5

Verse
Slowly and expressively

1. O come, O come Im - man - u - el, and
2., 3. *See additional lyrics*

ran - som cap - tive Is - ra - el, that mourns in lone - ly

ex - ile here un - til the Son of God _____ ap -

Chorus

pear. Re - joice, re - joice! Im - man - u -

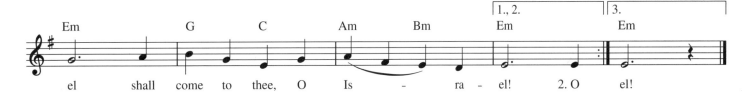

el shall come to thee, O Is - ra - el! 2. O el!

Additional Lyrics

2. O come Thou Wisdom from on high,
   And order all things far and nigh;
   To us the path of knowledge show,
   And cause us in her ways to go.

3. O come Desire of nations, bind
   All people in one heart and mind;
   Bid envy, strife, and quarrel's cease;
   Fill the whole world with heaven's peace.

O Little Town of Bethlehem

Words by Phillips Brooks
Music by Lewis H. Redner

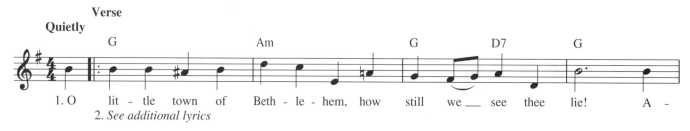

Strum Pattern: 4
Pick Pattern: 4, 5

Verse
Quietly

1. O lit - tle town of Beth - le - hem, how still we __ see thee lie! A -
2. *See additional lyrics*

bove thy deep and dream - less sleep, the si - lent __ stars go by; yet

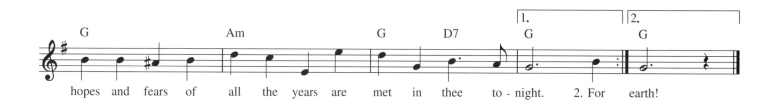

in thy dark streets shin - eth the ev - er - last - ing light; the

hopes and fears of all the years are met in thee to - night. 2. For earth!

Additional Lyrics

2. For Christ is born of Mary, and gathered all above.
   While mortals sleep the angels keep
   Their watch of wond'ring love.
   O morning stars, together proclaim the holy birth!
   And praises sing to God the King,
   And peace to men on earth!

Up on the Housetop

Words and Music by B.R. Handy

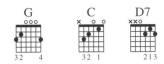

Strum Pattern: 4, 3
Pick Pattern: 4, 3

Verse
Brightly

1. Up on the house-top rein - deer pause, out jumps good old San - ta Claus;
2., 3. *See additional lyrics*

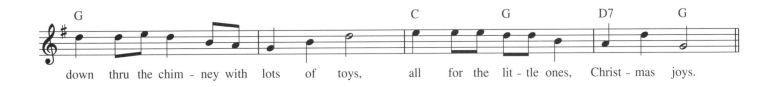

down thru the chim - ney with lots of toys, all for the lit - tle ones, Christ - mas joys.

Chorus

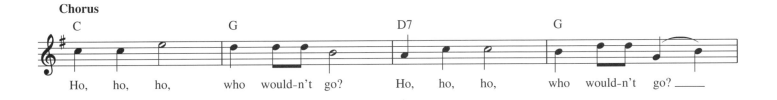

Ho, ho, ho, who would-n't go? Ho, ho, ho, who would-n't go? ___

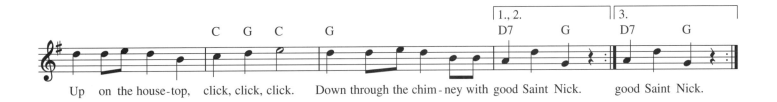

Up on the house-top, click, click, click. Down through the chim - ney with good Saint Nick. good Saint Nick.

Additional Lyrics

2. First comes the stocking of Little Nell,
   Oh, dear Santa, fill it well.
   Give her a dollie that laughs and cries,
   One that will open and shut her eyes.

3. Next comes the stocking of little Will,
   Oh, just see what a glorious fill!
   Here is a hammer and lots of tacks,
   Also a ball and a whip that cracks.

Please Come Home for Christmas

Words and Music by Charles Brown and Gene Redd

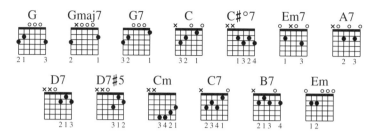

Strum Pattern: 8
Pick Pattern: 8

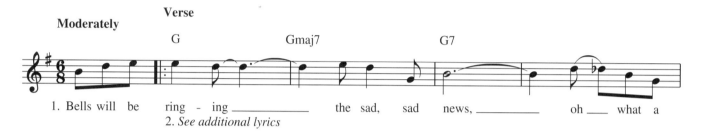

Moderately   **Verse**

G   Gmaj7   G7

1. Bells will be ring - ing _____ the sad, sad news, _____ oh _ what a
2. *See additional lyrics*

C   C#°7

Christ - mas _____ to have the blues! _____ My ba - by's

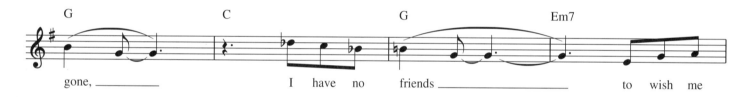

G   C   G   Em7

gone, _____ I have no friends _____ to wish me

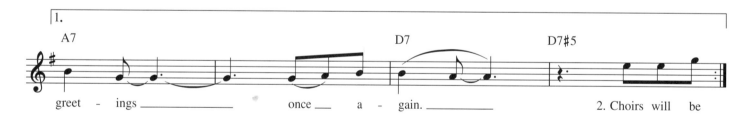

1.

A7   D7   D7#5

greet - ings _____ once _ a - gain. _____ 2. Choirs will be

2.

A7   D7   G   C   G   G7

Christ - mas, _ by New Year's night. _____ Friends and re -

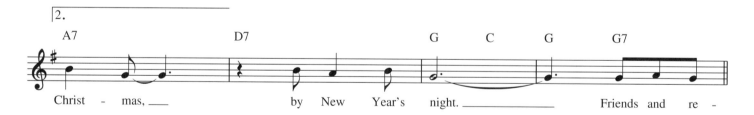

Bridge

C   Cm   G

la - tions _____ send sal - u - ta - tions _____ sure _ as the

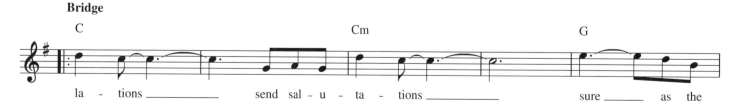

stars shine a - bove. _____ For this is Christ - mas, _____ yes, Christ - mas my

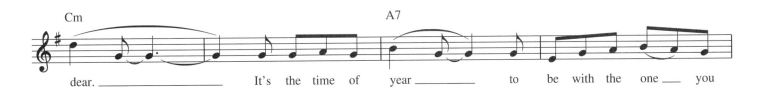

dear. _____ It's the time of year _____ to be with the one ___ you

Verse

love. 3., 4. So won't you tell me _____ you'll nev - er - more

roam, _____ Christ - mas and New Year _____ will find you at

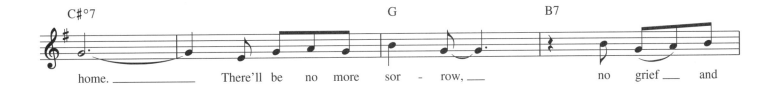

home. _____ There'll be no more sor - row, ___ no grief ___ and

pain _____ and I'll be hap - py, hap - py once _____ a -

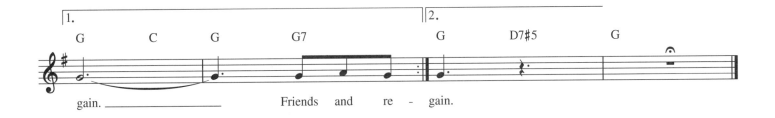

gain. _____ Friends and re - gain.

Additional Lyrics

2. Choirs will be singing "Silent Night,"
Christmas carols by candlelight.
Please come home for Christmas,
Please come home for Christmas;
If not for Christmas, by New Year's night.

Rudolph the Red-Nosed Reindeer

Music and Lyrics by Johnny Marks

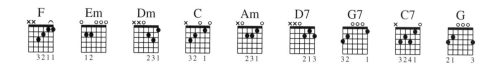

Intro
Freely

You know Dash-er and Danc-er and Pranc-er and Vix-en, Com-et and Cu-pid and

Don-ner and Blitz-en, but do you re-call the most fa-mous rein-deer of all?

Strum Pattern: 2, 3
Pick Pattern: 2, 3

Verse
Lightly

1., 2. Ru-dolph, the red-nosed rein-deer had a ver-y shin-y nose,

and if you ev-er saw it, you would e-ven say it glows.

All of the oth-er rein-deer used to laugh and call him names,

they nev - er let poor Ru - dolph join in an - y rein - deer games.

Bridge

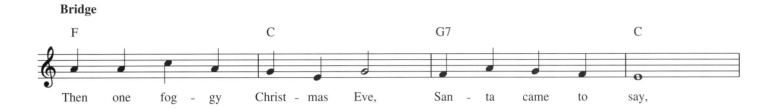

Then one fog - gy Christ - mas Eve, San - ta came to say,

"Ru - dolph, with your nose so bright, won't you guide my sleigh to - night?" _

Outro

Then how the rein - deer loved him as they shout - ed out with glee;

1.

"Ru-dolph, the red - nosed rein - deer, you'll go down in his - to - ry!"

2.

you'll go down in his - to - ry!" _____

We Wish You a Merry Christmas

Traditional English Folksong

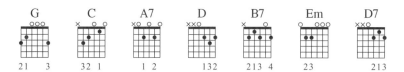

G   C   A7   D   B7   Em   D7

Strum Pattern: 8, 9
Pick Pattern: 8, 9

Verse
Brightly

1. We wish you a mer-ry Christ-mas. We wish you a mer-ry Christ-mas. We
2. *See additional lyrics*

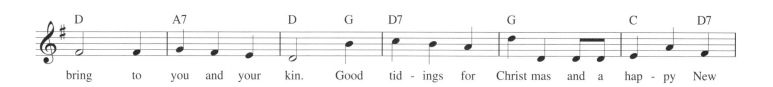

wish you a mer-ry Christ-mas and a hap-py New Year. Good tid-ings we

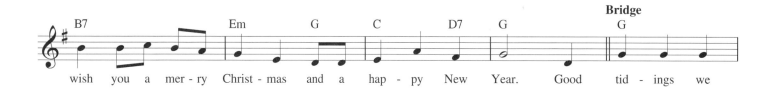

bring to you and your kin. Good tid-ings for Christ-mas and a hap-py New

Year. 2. We Year. 3. We wish you a mer-ry Christ-mas. We wish you a mer-ry

Christ-mas. We wish you a mer-ry Christ-mas and a hap-py New Year.

Additional Lyrics

2. We all know that Santa's coming.
   We all know that Santa's coming.
   We all know that Santa's coming.
   And soon will be here.

Where Are You Christmas?

from DR. SEUSS' HOW THE GRINCH STOLE CHRISTMAS

Words and Music by Will Jennings, James Horner and Mariah Carey

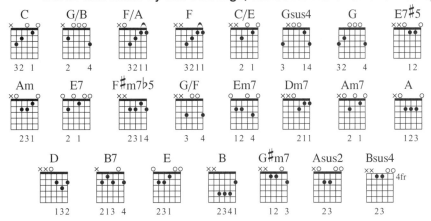

Strum Pattern: 2
Pick Pattern: 2, 4

Intro
Gently

1. Where are you,

Christ - mas? Why can't I find you? Why have you

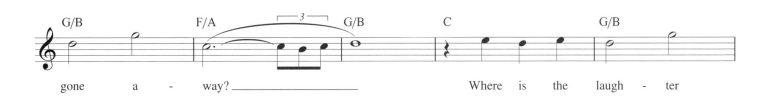

gone a - way? _____ Where is the laugh - ter

you used to bring me? Why can't I hear mu - sic play? _____

My world is chang - ing. ___ I'm re - ar -

rang - ing. Does that mean Christ - mas chang -

- es too? ___

Verse

2. Where are you, Christ - mas? Do you re - mem - ber the one you

used to know? ___ I'm not the

same one. _ See what the time's done. Is that why you ___ have

let ___ me go? ___ Oh, ___

Bridge

Christ - mas is here, _ ev - 'ry - where, ___ oh. ___

Blue Christmas

Words and Music by Billy Hayes and Jay Johnson

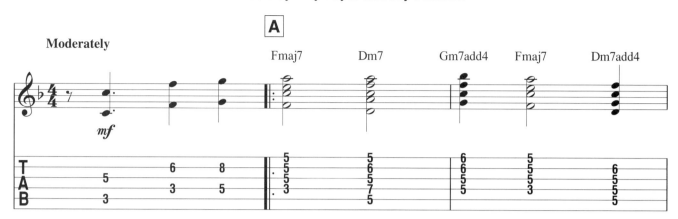

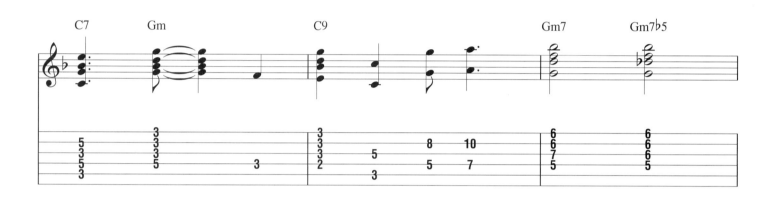

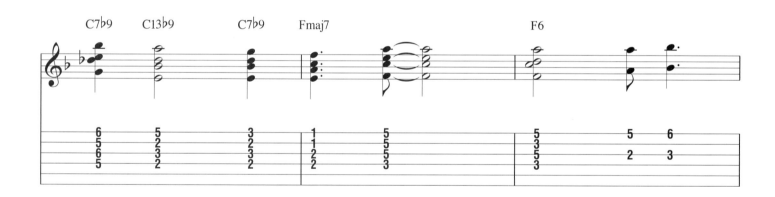

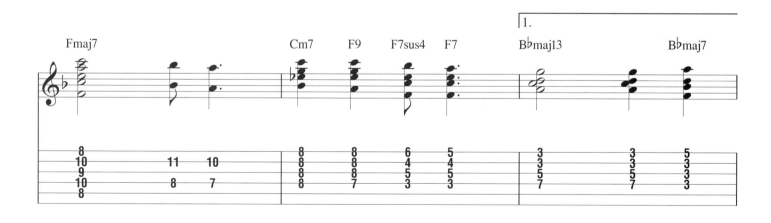

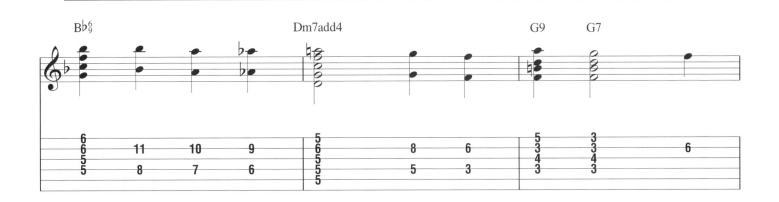

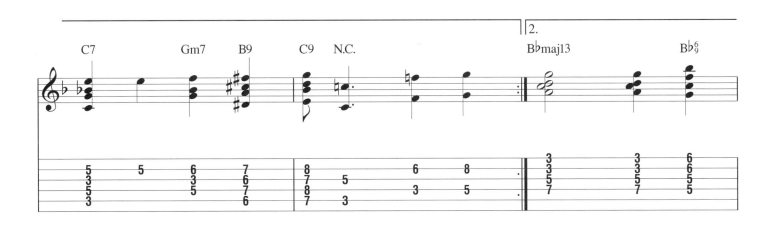

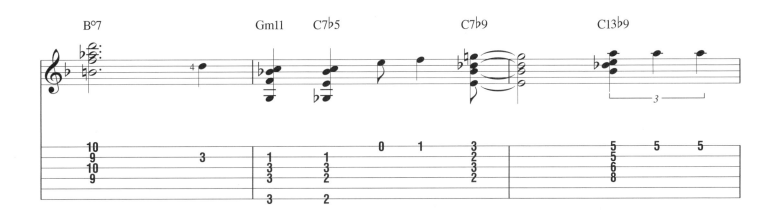

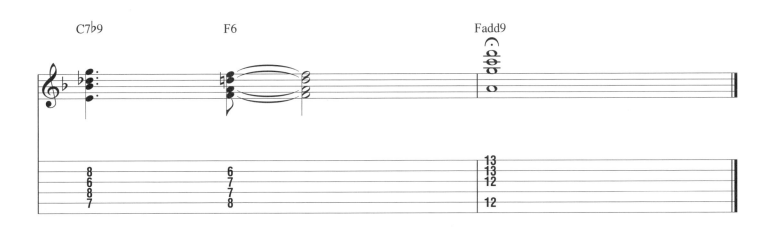

The Christmas Song

(Chestnuts Roasting on an Open Fire)

Music and Lyric by Mel Torme and Robert Wells

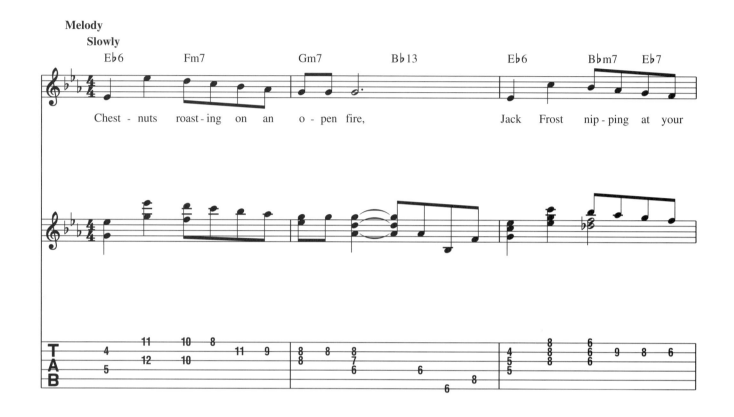

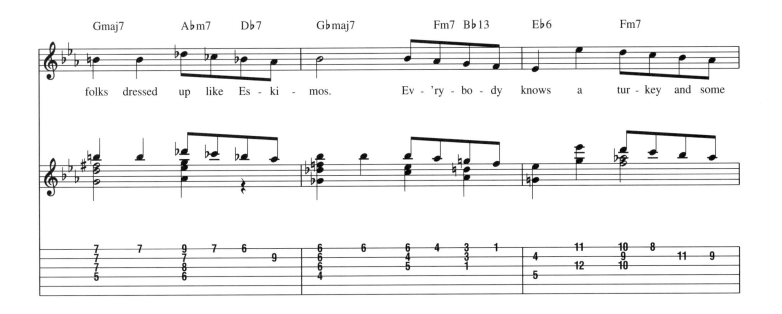

folks dressed up like Es - ki - mos. Ev - 'ry - bo - dy knows a tur - key and some

mis - tle - toe help to make the sea - son bright.

Ti - ny tots with their eyes all a - glow will find it hard to sleep to -

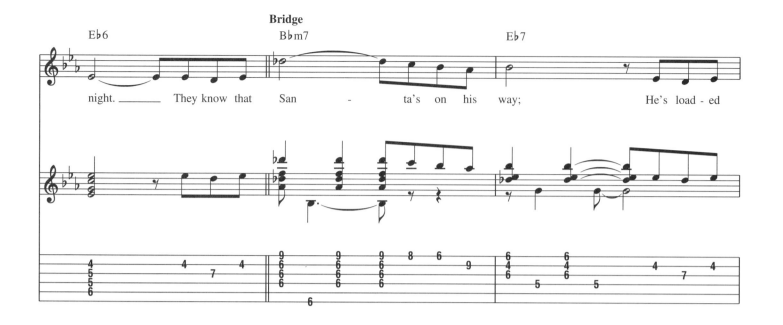

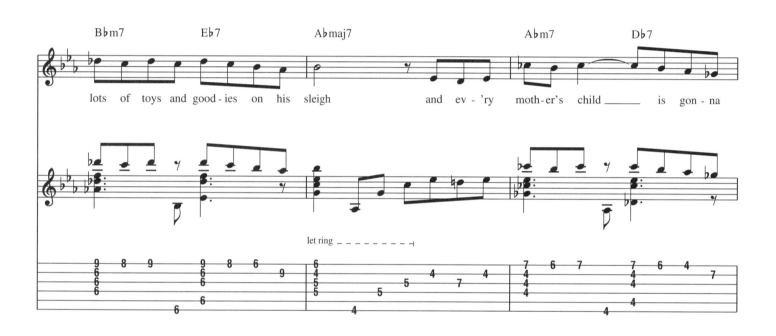

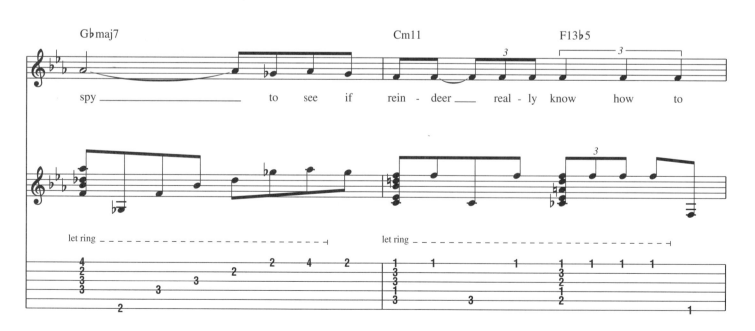

Melody

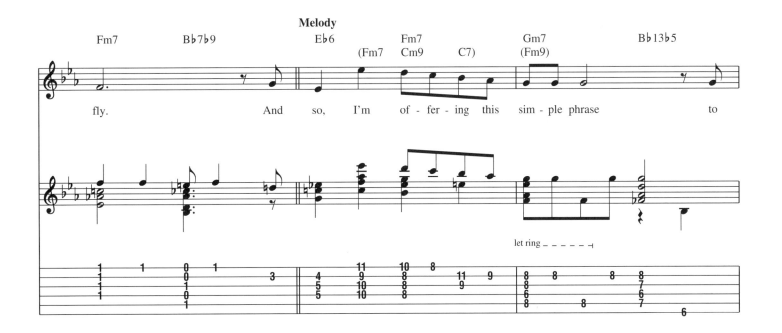

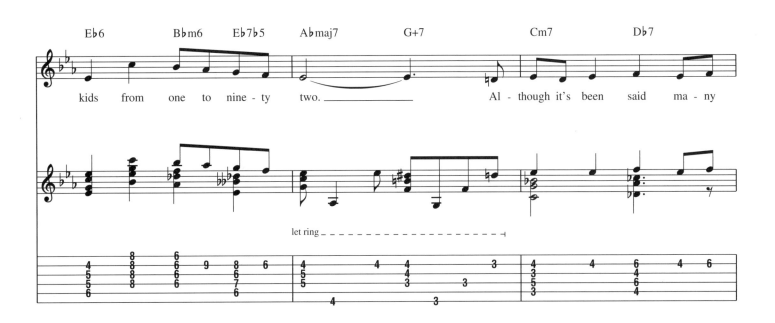

Happy Holiday

from the Motion Picture Irving Berlin's HOLIDAY INN

Words and Music by Irving Berlin

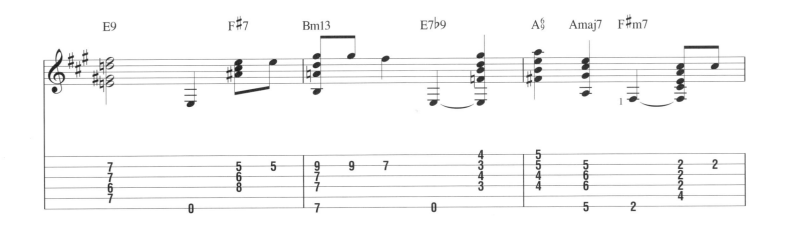

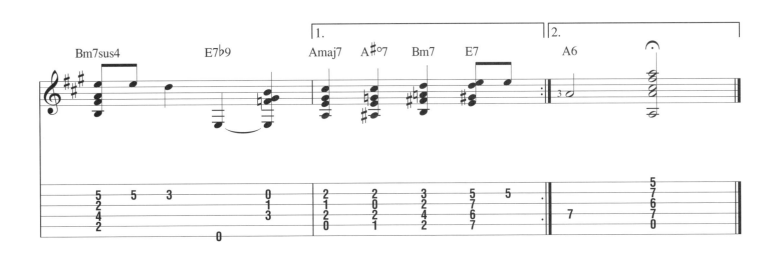

(There's No Place Like)
Home for the Holidays

Words by Al Stillman
Music by Robert Allen

Mistletoe and Holly

Words and Music by Frank Sinatra, Dok Stanford and Henry W. Sanicola

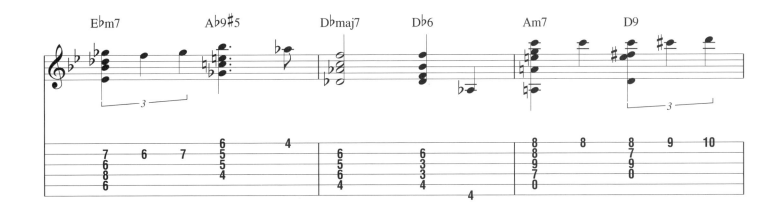

D.C. al Coda

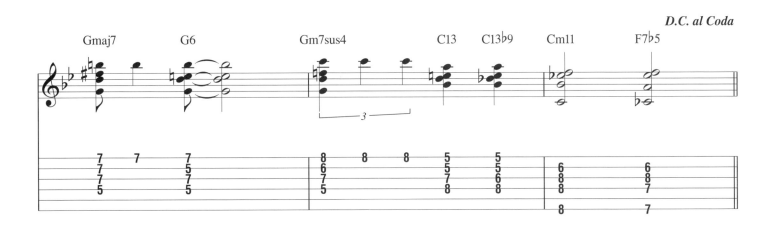

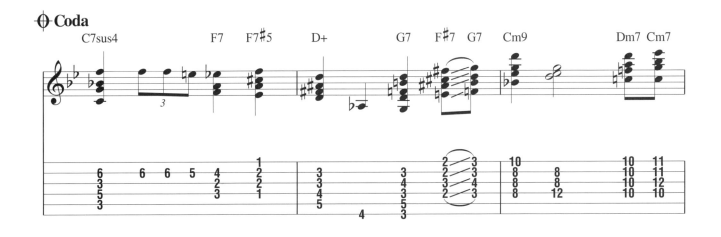

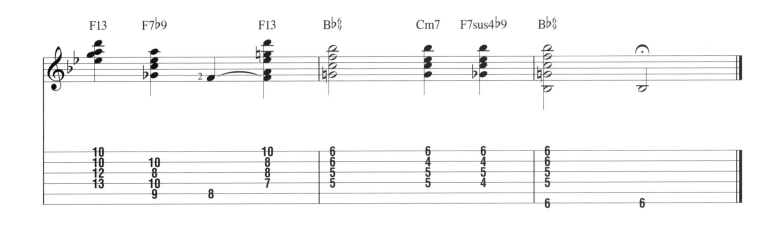

What Are You Doing New Year's Eve?

By Frank Loesser

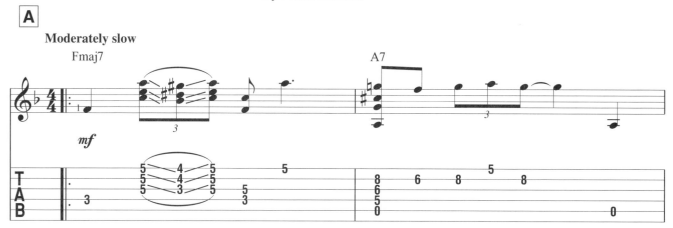

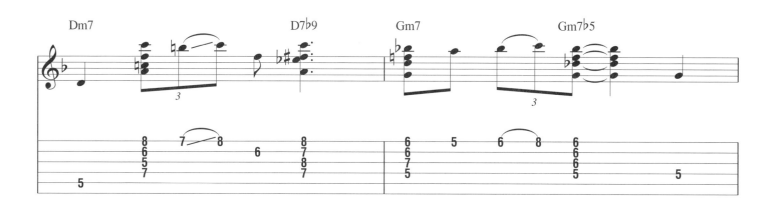

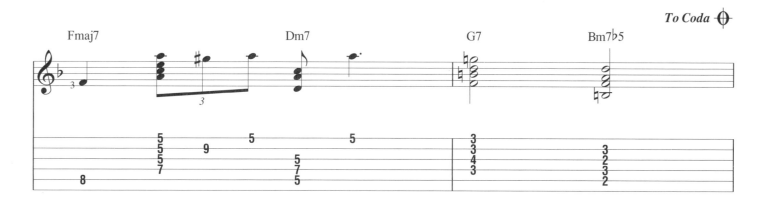

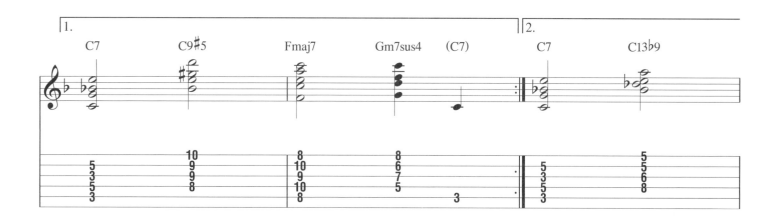

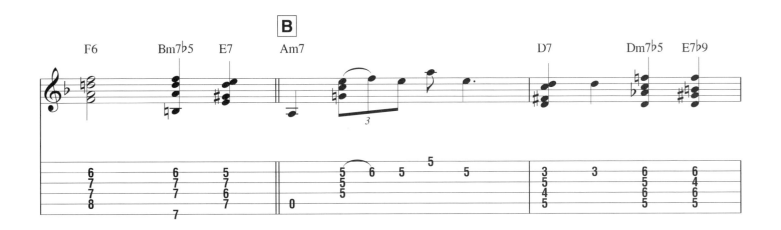

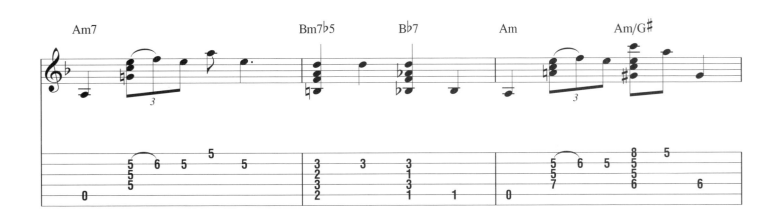

D.C. al Coda

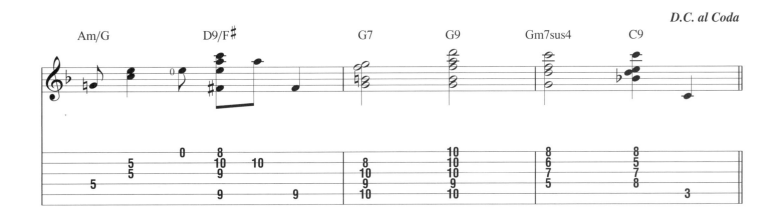

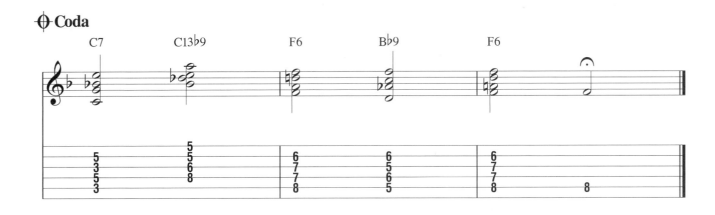

My Favorite Things

from THE SOUND OF MUSIC

Lyrics by Oscar Hammerstein II
Music by Richard Rodgers

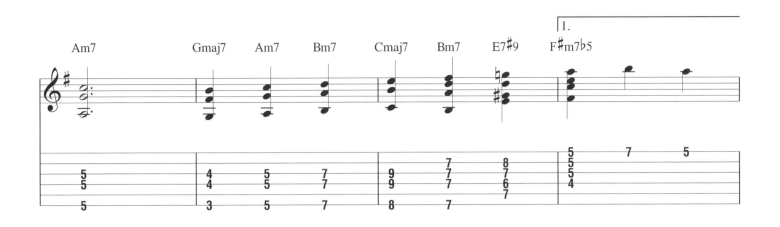

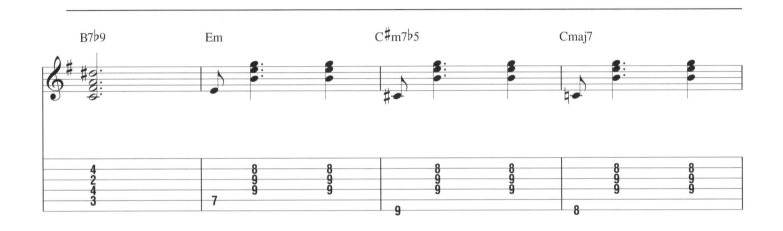

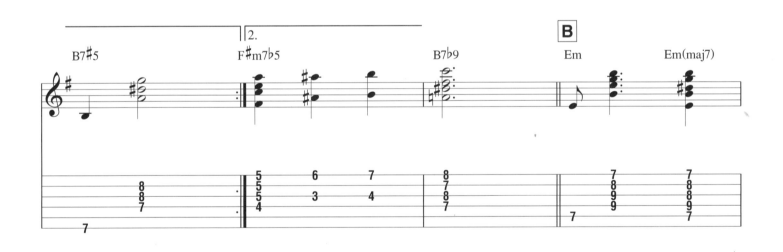

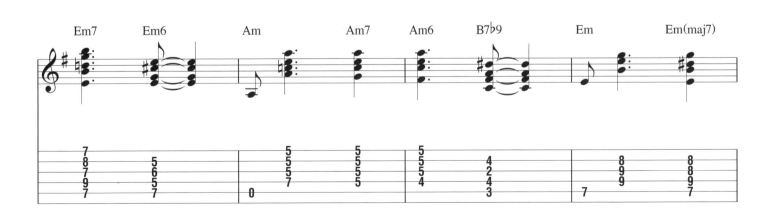

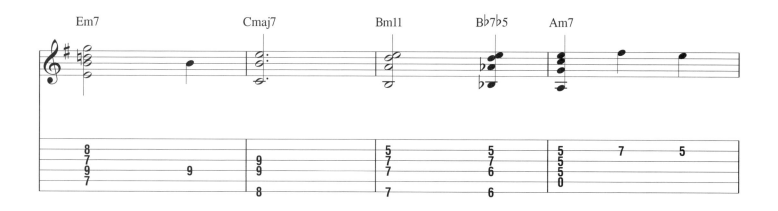

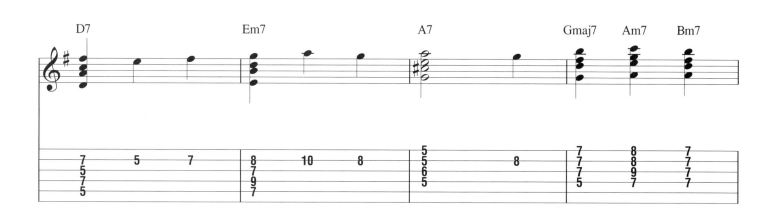

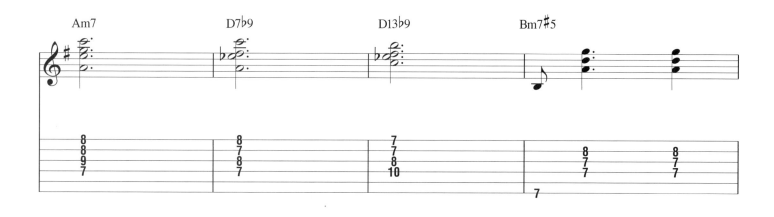

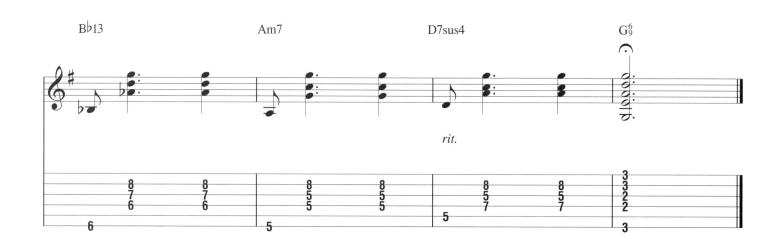

Canon in D

By Johann Pachelbel

Drop D tuning:
(low to high) D–A–D–G–B–E

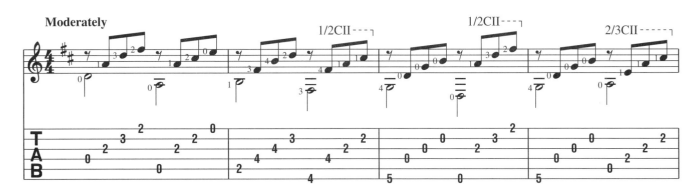

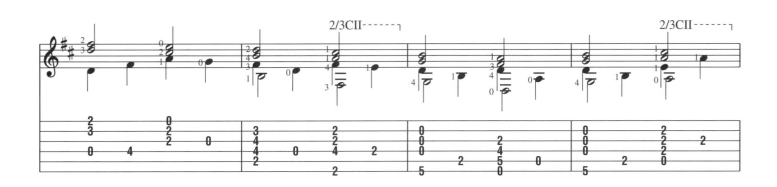

143

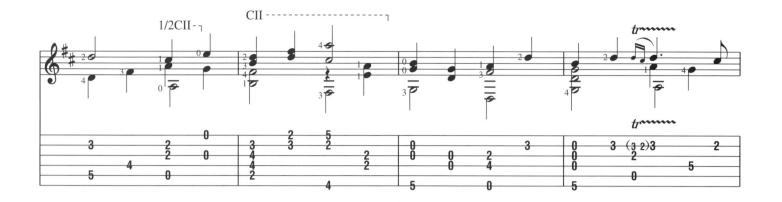

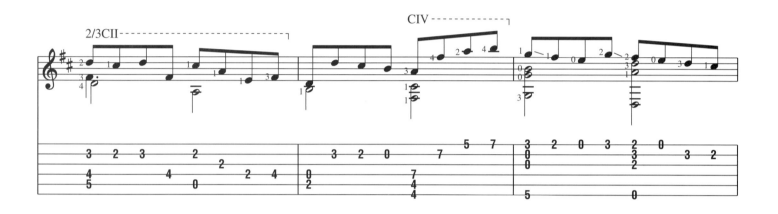

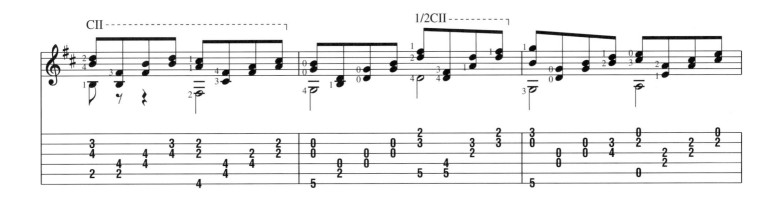

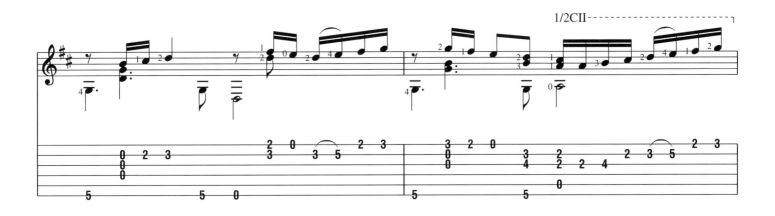

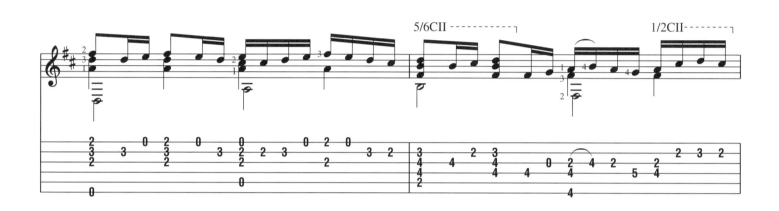

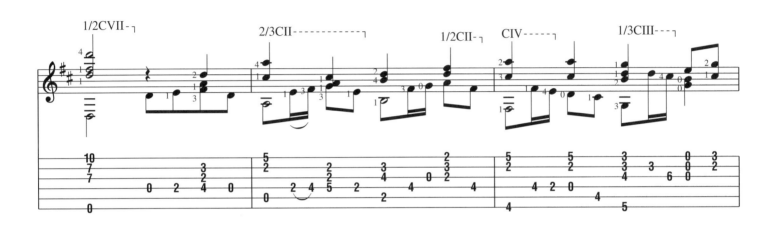

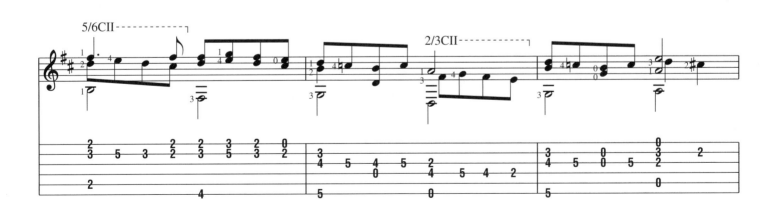

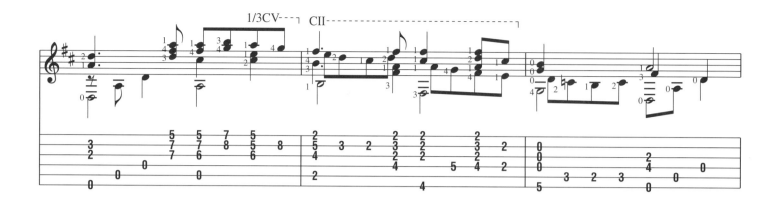

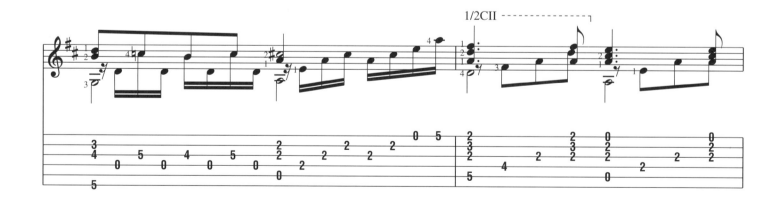

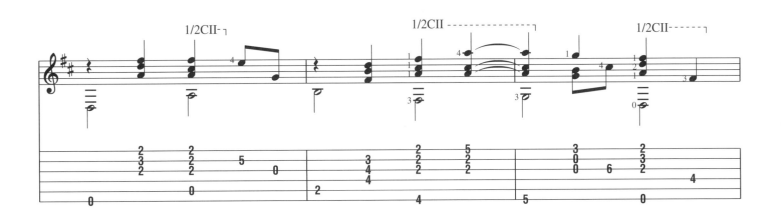

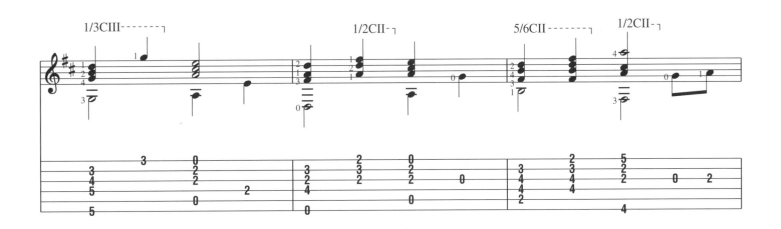

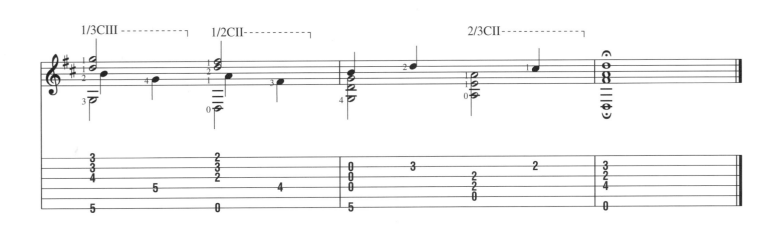

Ave Maria

By Franz Schubert

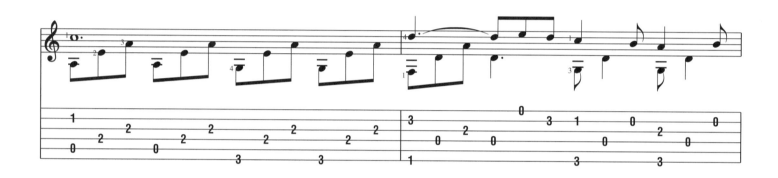

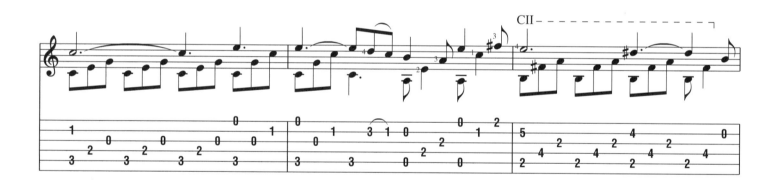

Jesu, Joy of Man's Desiring

English Words by Robert Bridges
Music by Johann Sebastian Bach

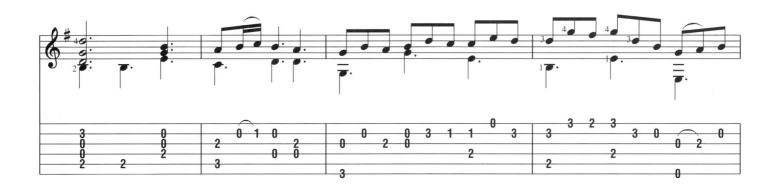

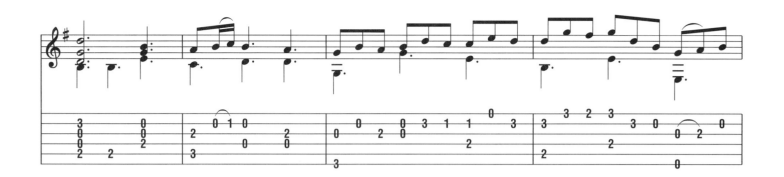

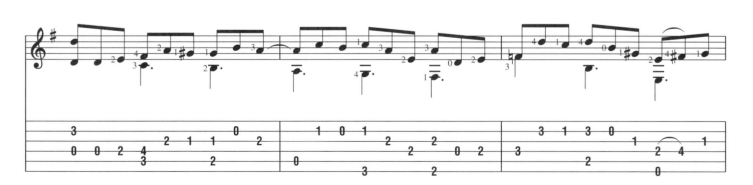

March

from THE NUTCRACKER

By Pyotr Il'yich Tchaikovsky

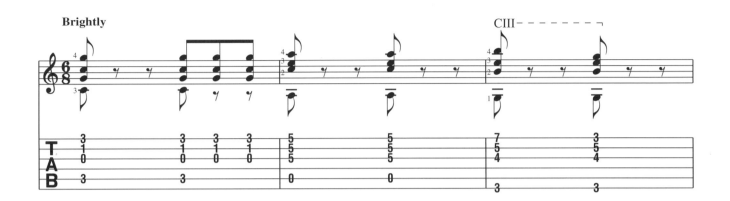

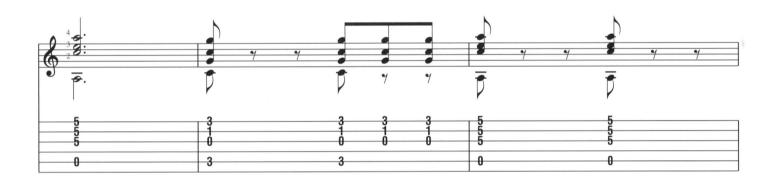

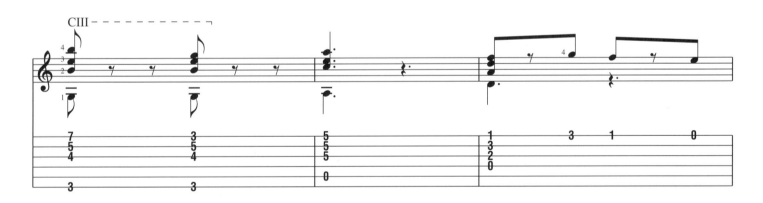

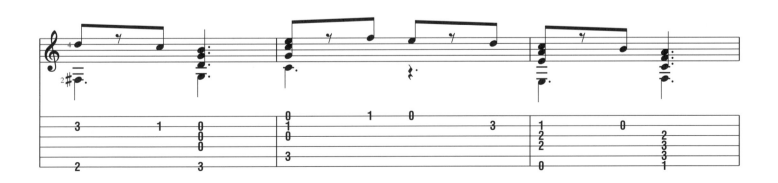

Sheep May Safely Graze

By Johann Sebastian Bach

Drop D tuning:
(low to high) D-A-D-G-B-E

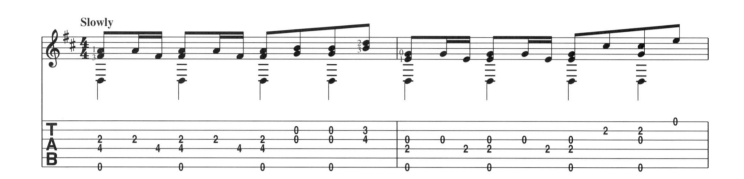

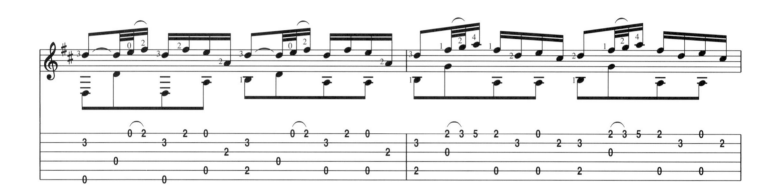

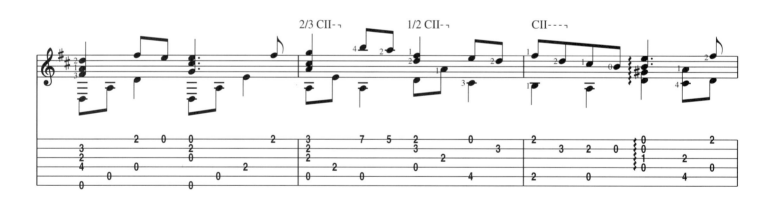

What Child Is This?

Words by William C. Dix
16th Century English Melody

Slowly

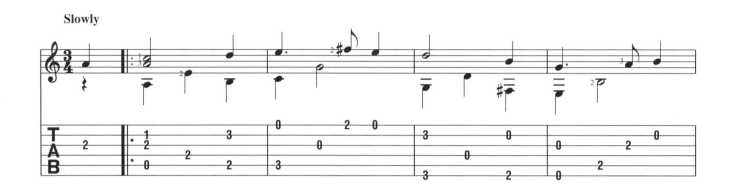

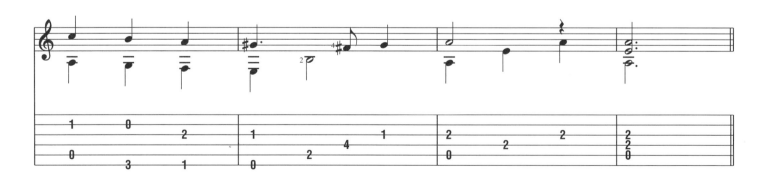

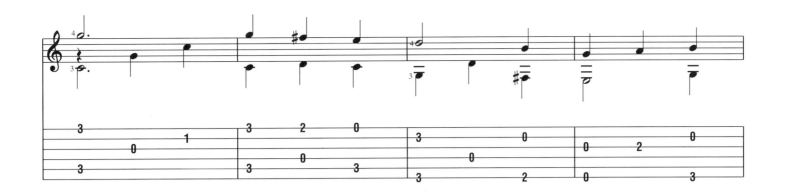

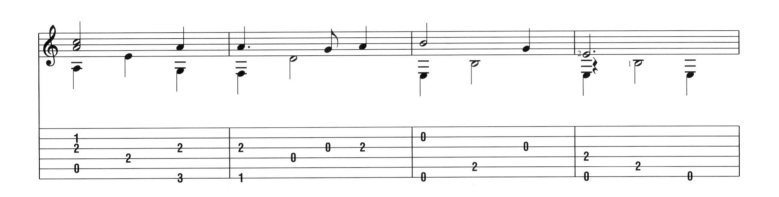

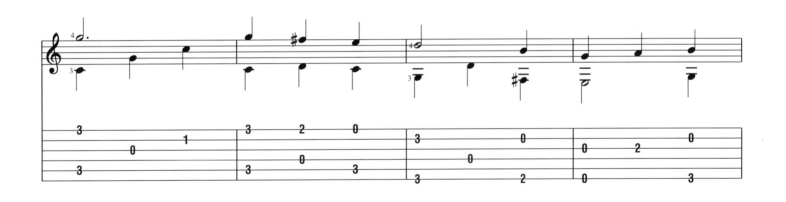

Do You Hear What I Hear

Words and Music by Noel Regney and Gloria Shayne

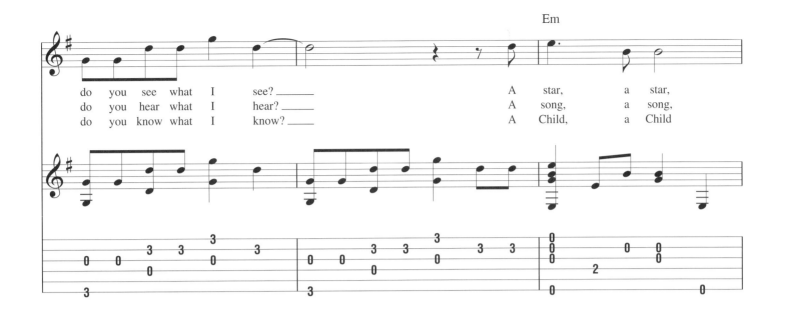

do you see what I see? _____
do you hear what I hear? _____
do you know what I know? _____

A star, a star,
A song, a song,
A Child, a Child

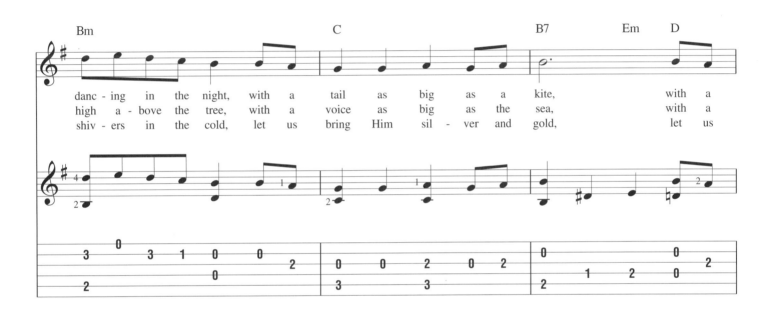

danc - ing in the night, with a tail as big as a kite, with a
high a - bove the tree, with a voice as big as the sea, with a
shiv - ers in the cold, let us bring Him sil - ver and gold, let us

tail as big as a kite."
voice as big as the sea."
bring Him sil - ver and gold."

2. Said the
3. Said the

165

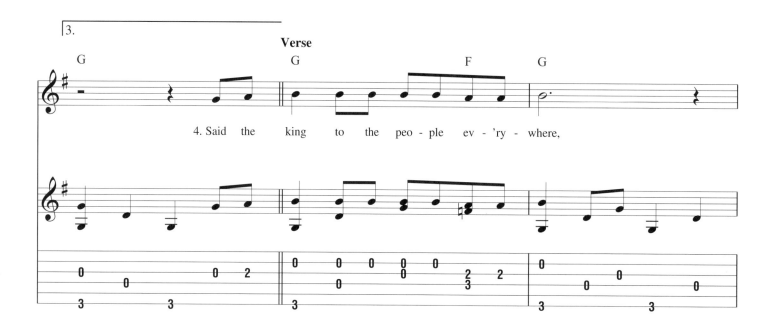

4. Said the king to the peo - ple ev - 'ry - where,

"Lis - ten to what I say! _____ Pray for peace, peo - ple ev - 'ry -

where, lis - ten to what I say! _____ The

Child,   the Child,   sleep - ing in the night, He will bring us good - ness and

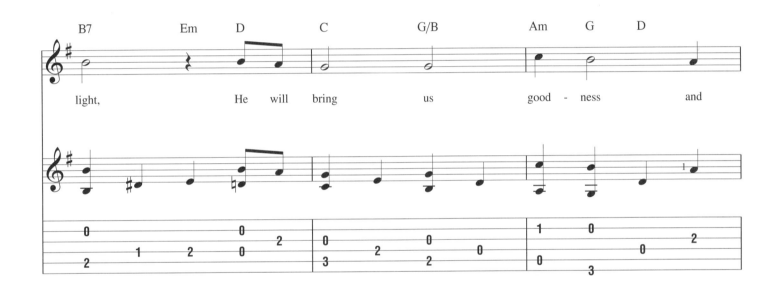

light,   He will bring   us   good - ness   and

light." _____

God Rest Ye Merry, Gentlmen

19th Century English Carol

Verse
Moderately

1. God rest ye mer - ry, gen - tle - men, let noth - ing you dis -
Beth - le - hem, in Jew - ry, this bless - ed babe was
God, our Heav'n - ly Fath - er, a bless - ed an - gel

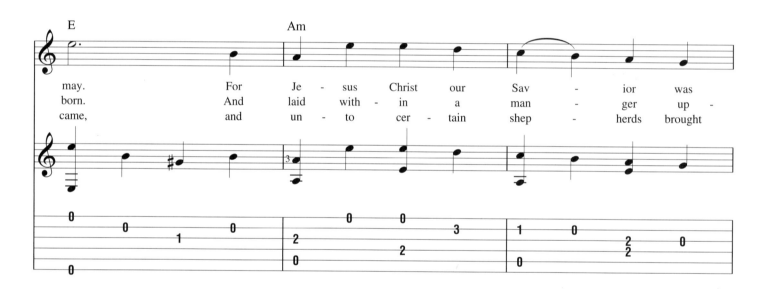

may. For Je - sus Christ our Sav - ior was
born. And laid with - in a man - ger up -
came, and un - to cer - tain shep - herds brought

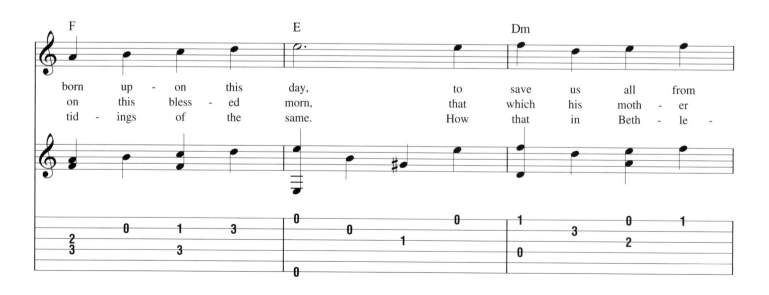

born up - on this day, to save us all from
on this bless - ed morn, that which his moth - er
tid - ings of the same. How that in Beth - le -

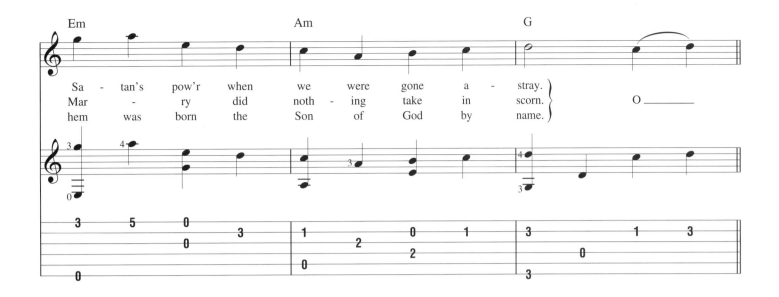

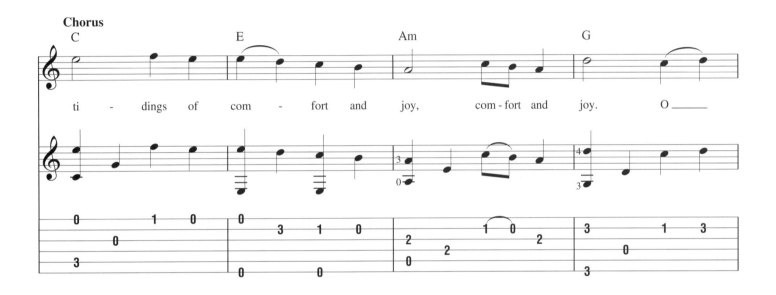

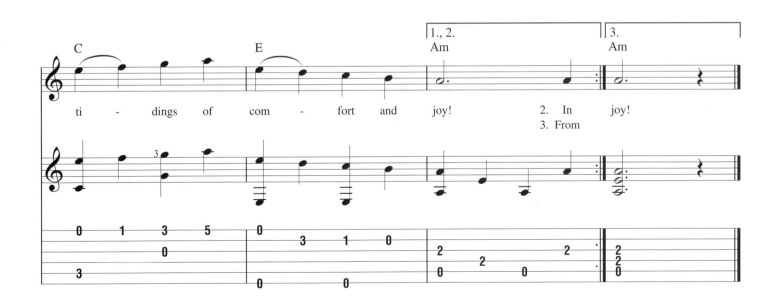

It Came Upon the Midnight Clear

Words by Edmund Hamilton Sears
Music by Richard Storrs Willis

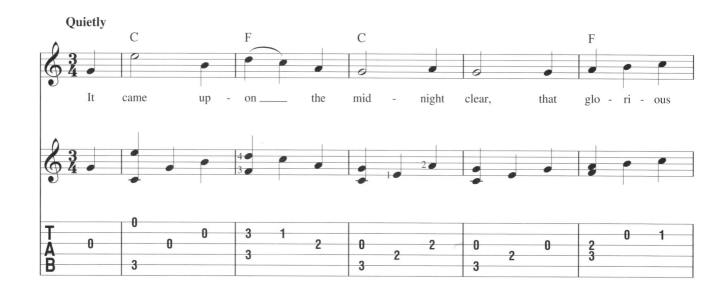

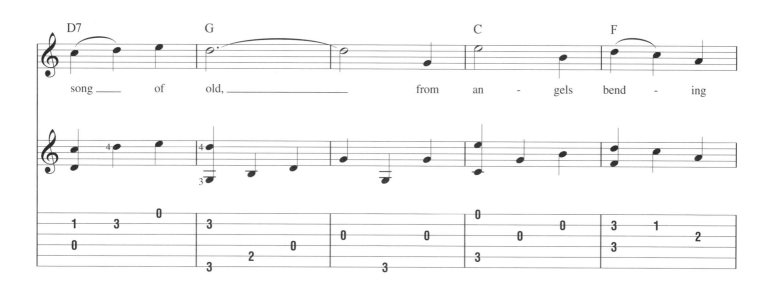

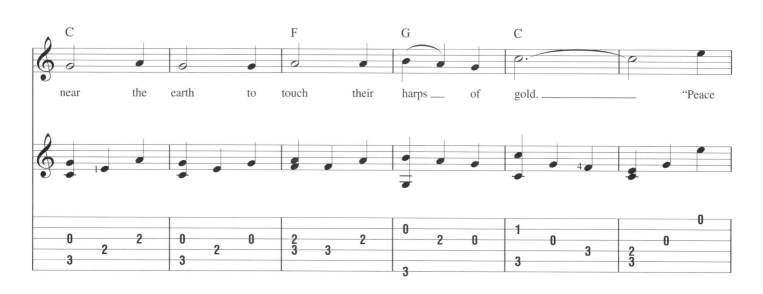

on the earth, ___ good will to men, from heav - en's all -

gra - cious King." _____ The world in sol - emn

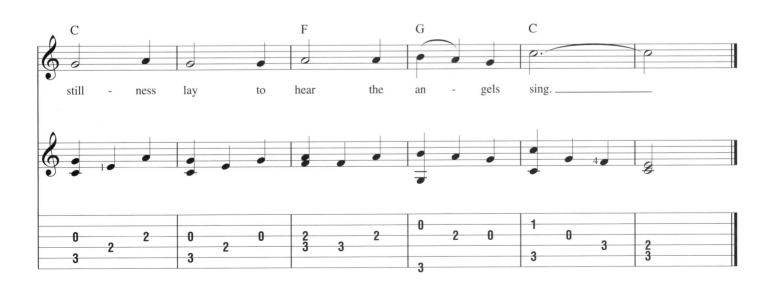

still - ness lay to hear the an - gels sing. _____

Let It Snow! Let It Snow! Let It Snow!

Words by Sammy Cahn
Music by Jule Styne

Bridge

fin - al - ly kiss good - night, how I'll hate go - ing out in the

storm. But if you'll real - ly hold me tight,

D.S. al Coda

Coda

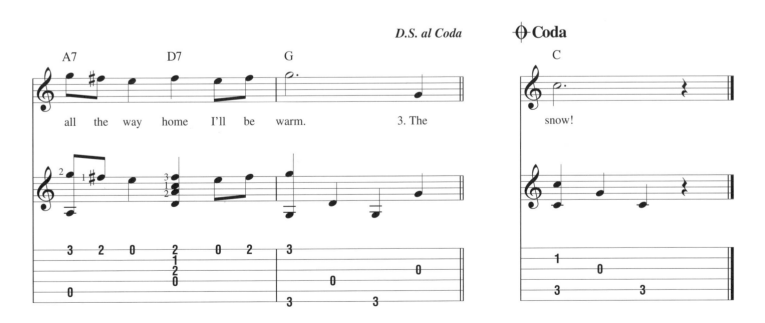

all the way home I'll be warm. 3. The

snow!

Silver Bells

from the Paramount Picture THE LEMON DROP KID

Words and Music by Jay Livingston and Ray Evans

Verse

Moderately

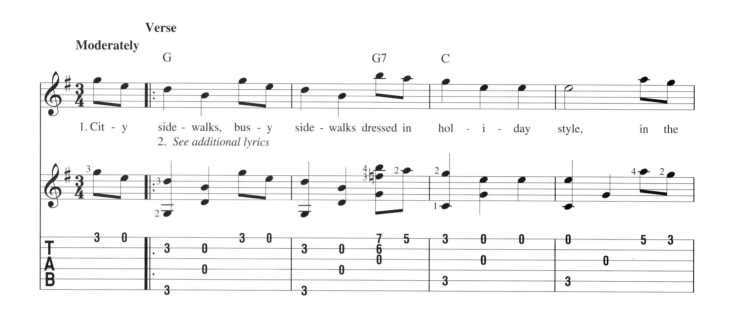

1. Cit - y side - walks, bus - y side - walks dressed in hol - i - day style, in the
2. *See additional lyrics*

air there's a feel - ing ___ of Christ - mas. ___ Chil - dren laugh - ing, peo - ple pass - ing, meet - ing

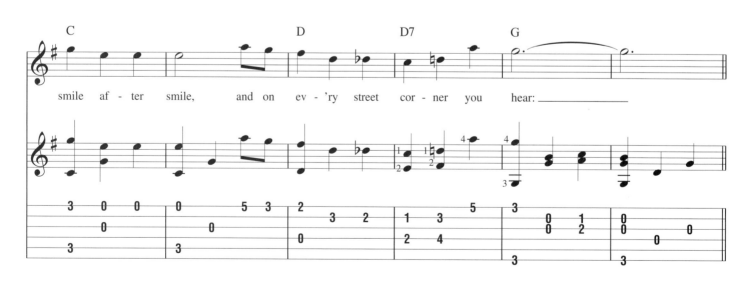

smile af - ter smile, and on ev - 'ry street cor - ner you hear: ___

Chorus

Additional Lyrics

2. Strings of street lights, even stop lights
   Blink a bright red and green,
   As the shoppers rush home with their treasures.
   Hear the snow crunch, see the kids bunch,
   This is Santa's big scene.
   And above all the bustle you hear:

This Christmas

Words and Music by Donny Hathaway and Nadine McKinnor

Intro
Moderately

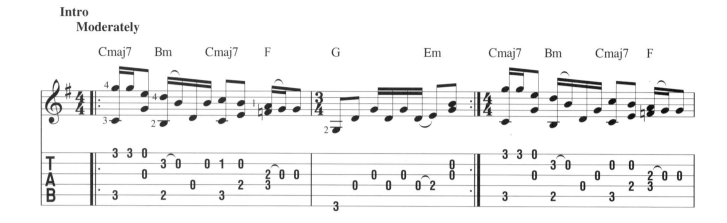

Verse

1. Hang all the mis-tle-toe. __ I'm gon-na get to know you
2. Pres-ents and cards are here. __ My world is filled with cheer and

bet-ter, _____ this Christ-mas. And as we trim the tree, __
you, _____ this Christ-mas. And as I look a-round, _

how much fun it's gon - na be to - geth - er, _____ this Christ - mas.
your __ eyes out - shine the town; they do, _____ this Christ - mas. } The

Chorus

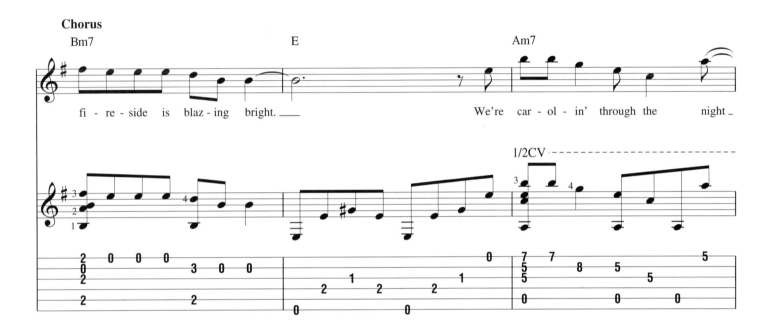

fi - re - side is blaz - ing bright. ____ We're car - ol - in' through the night _

_____ and this Christ - mas will be a ver - y spe - cial

Shake your hand, shake your hand now. _____

Wish your broth - er mer - ry Christ - mas _____

all o - ver the land now.

Outro

We Three Kings of Orient Are

Words and Music by John H. Hopkins, Jr.

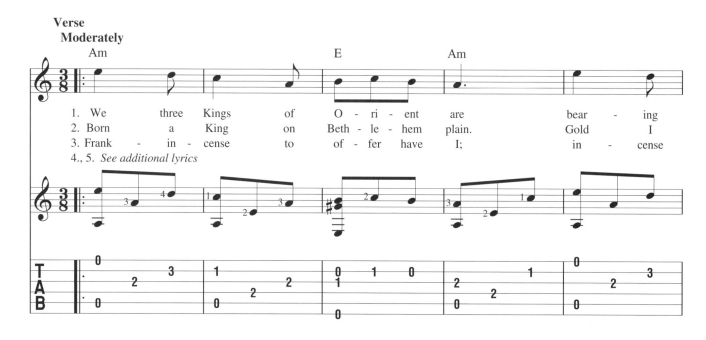

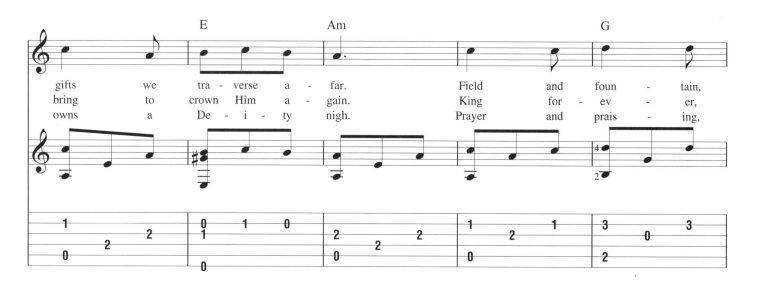

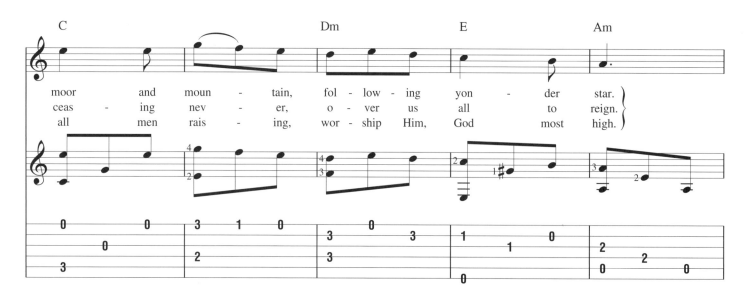

Chorus

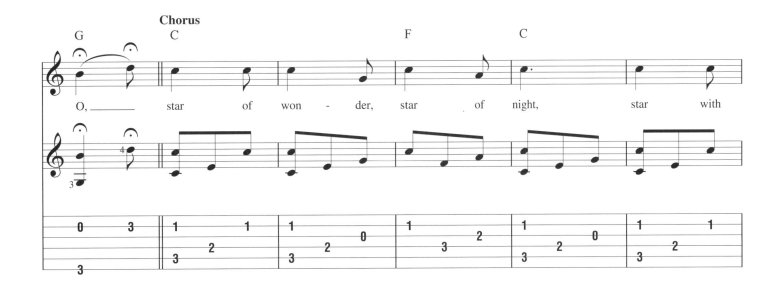

O, _____ star of won - der, star of night, star with

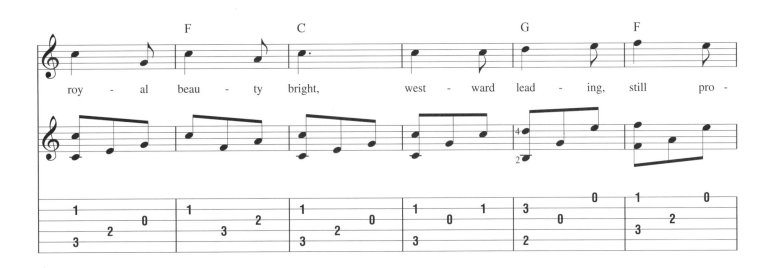

roy - al beau - ty bright, west - ward lead - ing, still pro -

ceed - ing, guide us to thy per - fect light. light.

Additional Lyrics

4. Myrrh is mine: its bitter perfume
   Breathes a life of gathering gloom.
   Sorrowing, sighing, bleeding, dying;
   Sealed in the stone-cold tomb.

5. Glorious now, behold Him arise,
   King and God, and Sacrifice!
   Heav'n sings alleluia,
   Alleluia, the earth replies:

I Saw Three Ships

Traditional English Carol

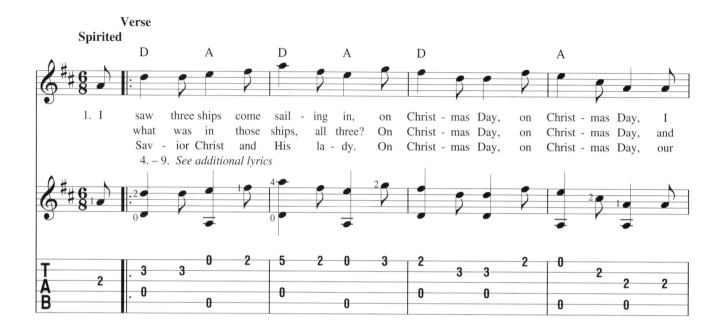

Verse
Spirited

1. I saw three ships come sail - ing in, on Christ - mas Day, on Christ - mas Day, I
   what was in those ships, all three? On Christ - mas Day, on Christ - mas Day, and
   Sav - ior Christ and His la - dy. On Christ - mas Day, on Christ - mas Day, our

4. – 9. *See additional lyrics*

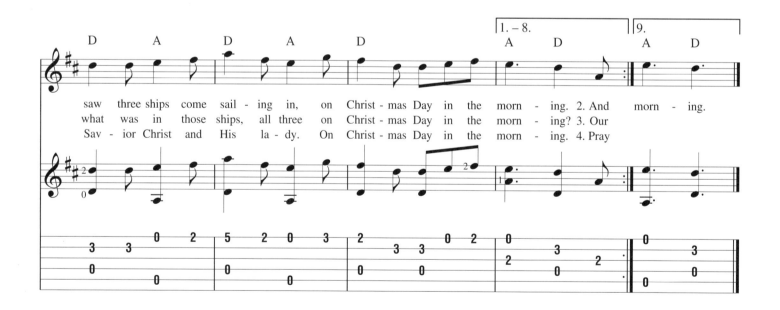

saw three ships come sail - ing in, on Christ - mas Day in the morn - ing. 2. And morn - ing.
what was in those ships, all three on Christ - mas Day in the morn - ing? 3. Our
Sav - ior Christ and His la - dy. On Christ - mas Day in the morn - ing. 4. Pray

Additional Lyrics

4. Pray, whither sailed those ships all three?
5. O, they sailed into Bethlehem.
6. And all the bells on earth shall ring,
7. And all the angels in heaven sing,
8. And all the souls on earth shall sing,
9. Then let us all rejoice again!

Bring a Torch, Jeannette, Isabella

17th Century French Provençal Carol

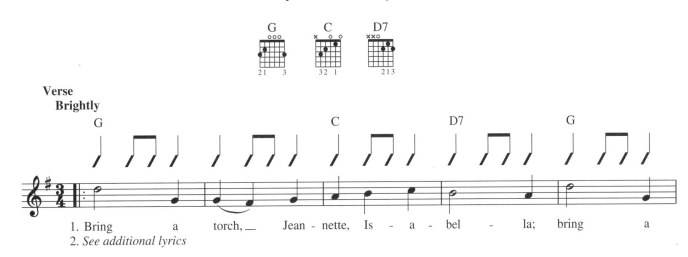

Verse
Brightly

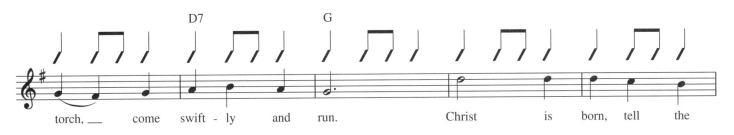

1. Bring a torch, __ Jean - nette, Is - a - bel - la; bring a
2. *See additional lyrics*

torch, __ come swift - ly and run. Christ is born, tell the

folk of the vil - lage, Je - sus is sleep - ing in His cra - dle.

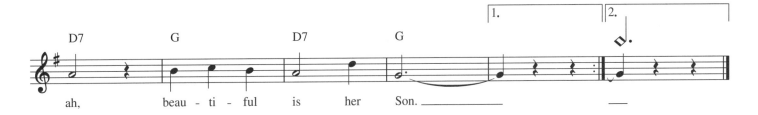

Ah, ah, beau - ti - ful is the Moth - er. Ah,

ah, beau - ti - ful is her Son. __

Additional Lyrics

2. Hasten now, good folk of the village,
Hasten now, the Christ Child to see.
You will find him asleep in a manger,
Quietly come and whisper softly.
Hush, hush, peacefully how He slumbers,
Hush, hush, peacefully how He sleeps.

Coventry Carol

Words by Robert Croo
Traditional English Melody

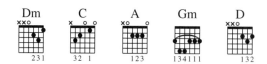

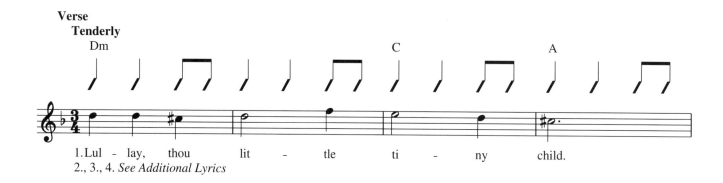

Verse
Tenderly

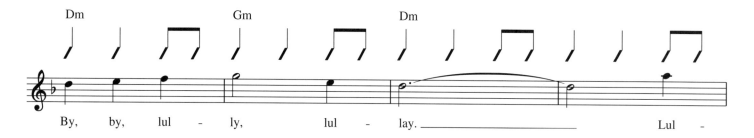

1. Lul - lay, thou lit - tle ti - ny child.
2., 3., 4. *See Additional Lyrics*

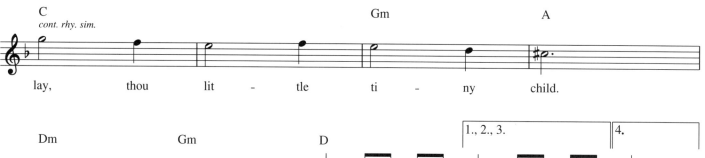

By, by, lul - ly, lul - lay. _____ Lul -

lay, thou lit - tle ti - ny child.

By, by, lul - ly, lul - lay. _____

Additional Lyrics

2. Oh, sisters too,
   How may we do,
   For to preserve this day?
   This poor youngling,
   For whom we sing
   By, by, lully lullay.

3. Herod the king,
   In his raging,
   Charged he hath this day.
   His men of might,
   In his own sight,
   All young children to slay.

4. That woe is me,
   Poor child for thee!
   And ever morn and day,
   For thy parting
   Neither say nor sing
   By, by, lully lullay!

Dance of the Sugar Plum Fairy

from THE NUTCRACKER

By Pyotr Il'yich Tchaikovsky

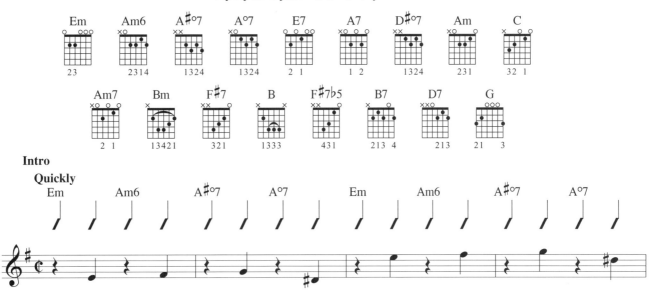

Intro

Quickly

Do They Know It's Christmas?

Words and Music by M. Ure and B. Geldof

But say a prayer, to pray for the oth-er ones ____

____ at Christ-mas-time. It's hard, but ____ when you're hav-ing fun ____

____ there's ____ a ____ world out-side your win - dow, ____ and it's a

world of ____ dread and fear ____ where the on - ly wa - ter

flow - ing is ____ the bit - ter sting of tears. And the

Christ-mas bells ____ that ring ____ there ____ are the clang-ing chimes of doom. ____

Well, to-night thank God it's them ____ in - stead of you. ____

And there won't be snow ____ in Af - ri - ca ____ this Christ -

- mas - time, ____ the great-est gift ____ they'll

Fum, Fum, Fum

Traditional Catalonian Carol

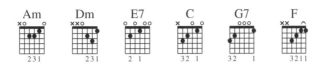

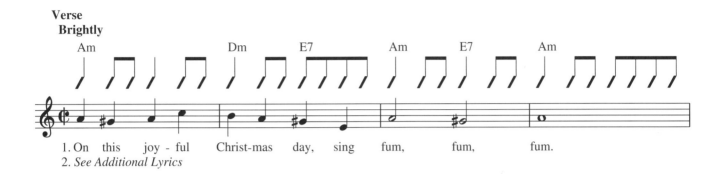

Verse
Brightly

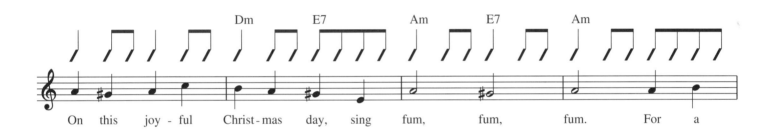

1. On this joy - ful Christ-mas day, sing fum, fum, fum.
2. *See Additional Lyrics*

On this joy - ful Christ-mas day, sing fum, fum, fum. For a

cont. rhy. sim.

bless - ed babe was born up - on this day at break of morn. In a man - ger poor and

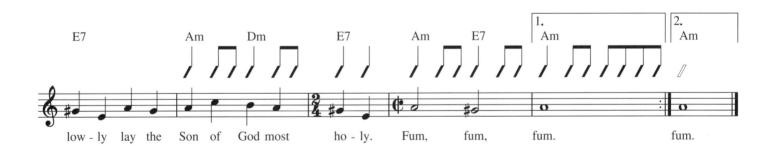

low - ly lay the Son of God most ho - ly. Fum, fum, fum. fum.

Additional Lyrics

2. Thanks to God for holidays, sing fum, fum, fum.
   Thanks to God for holidays, sing fum, fum, fum.
   Now we all our voices raise.
   And sing a song of grateful praise.
   Celebrate in song and story, all the wonders of his glory.
   Fum, fum, fum.

Go, Tell It on the Mountain

African-American Spiritual
Verses by John W. Work, Jr.

Additional Lyrics

2. The shepherds feared and trembled
When, lo! above the earth
Rang out the angel chorus
That hailed our Savior's birth.

3. Down in a lowly manger
Our humble Christ was born.
And God sent us salvation
That blessed Christmas morn.

Jesus Is Born

Words and Music by Steve Green, Phil Naish and Colleen Green

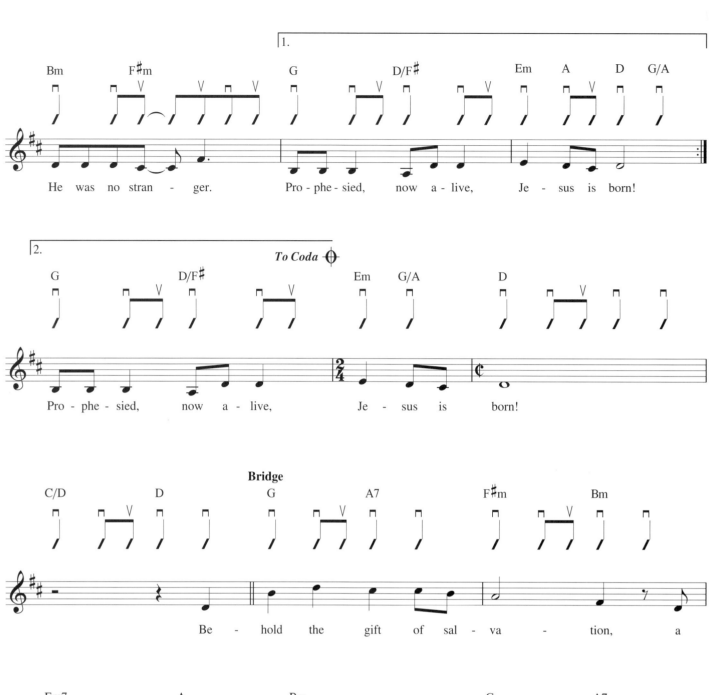

He was no stran - ger. Pro - phe - sied, now a - live, Je - sus is born!

Pro - phe - sied, now a - live, Je - sus is born!

Bridge

Be - hold the gift of sal - va - tion, a

light for ___ all to see, re - veal - ing all God's

glo - ry, Em - man - u - el is he. ___

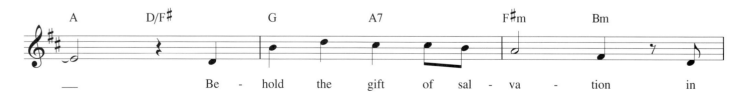

___ Be - hold the gift of sal - va - tion in

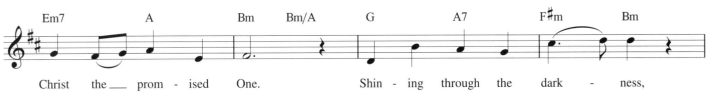

Christ the __ prom - ised One.   Shin - ing through the dark - ness,

D.S. al Coda
(take 2nd ending)

Je - sus   Christ   has   come. _____

Coda   **Verse**

Je - sus is born!   4. The bells are ring - ing,   peo - ple are sing - ing,

an - gels   say with joy,   "Je - sus is born!"   There in a man - ger,

He was no stran - ger.   Pro - phe - sied, now a - live,   Je - sus is born!

Bridge

Glo - ry to __ the King,   Lord of ev - 'ry - thing,

Christ has fi - nal - ly come. Glo - ry to___ the King, let the peo - ple sing

Hal - le - lu - jah,_____ Hal - le - lu - jah._____

Verse

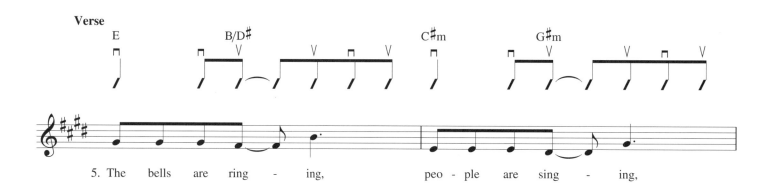

5. The bells are ring - ing, peo - ple are sing - ing,

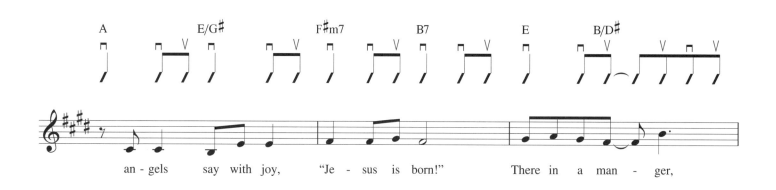

an - gels say with joy, "Je - sus is born!" There in a man - ger,

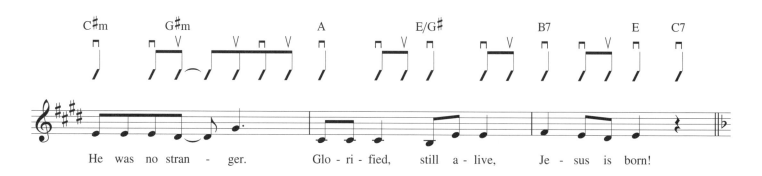

He was no stran - ger. Glo - ri - fied, still a - live, Je - sus is born!

Verse

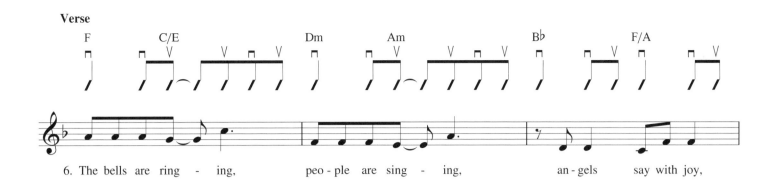

6. The bells are ring - ing, peo - ple are sing - ing, an - gels say with joy,

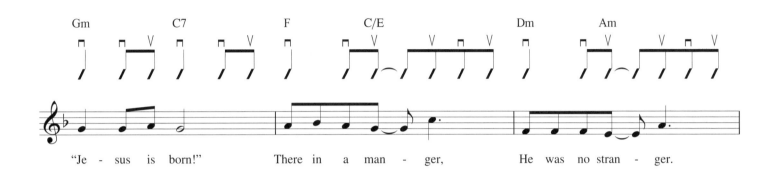

"Je - sus is born!" There in a man - ger, He was no stran - ger.

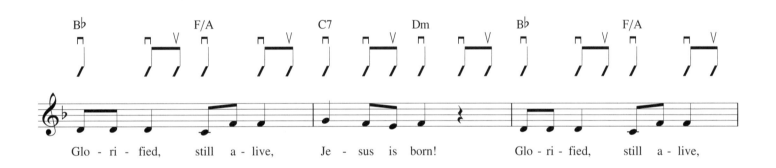

Glo - ri - fied, still a - live, Je - sus is born! Glo - ri - fied, still a - live,

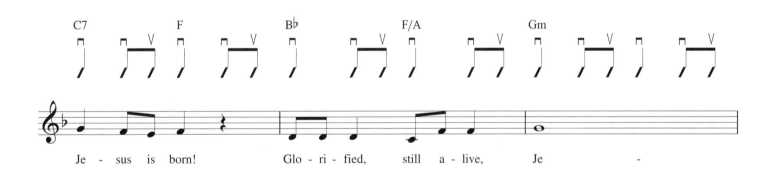

Je - sus is born! Glo - ri - fied, still a - live, Je -

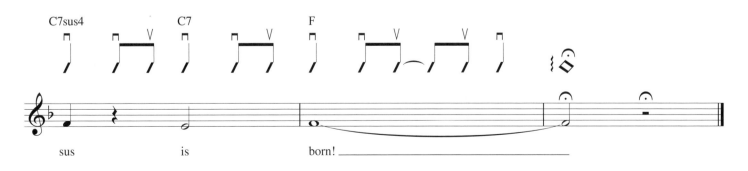

sus is born! _____

Grandma Got Run Over by a Reindeer

Words and Music by Randy Brooks

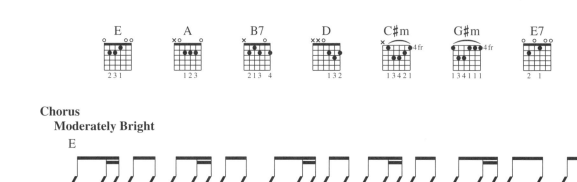

E   A   B7   D   C#m   G#m   E7

Chorus
Moderately Bright

Grand-ma got run o-ver by a rein-deer   walk-ing home from our house Christ-mas

Eve.   You can   say there's no such thing as   San-ta,   but

To Coda ⊕   **Verse**

as   for   me and Grand-pa,   we   be-lieve.   1. She'd been drink-ing   too much
2., 3. *See Additional Lyrics*

egg-nog   and   we begged her   not   to   go.

But   she for-got her med-i-ca-tion,   and   she   stag-gered out the door in-to the

snow. When we found her Christ-mas morn-ing

at the scene of the at-tack, she had hoof-prints on her

1., 2. **3.** *D.C. al Coda*

fore-head, and in-crim-i-nat-ing Claus marks on her back. elves.

Coda

Outro-Chorus

lieve. Grand-ma got run o-ver by a rein-deer

walk-ing home from our house Christ-mas Eve. You can say there's no such thing as

San-ta, but as for me and Grand-pa, we be-lieve. _____

Additional Lyrics

2. Now we're all so proud of Grandpa.
He's been taking it so well.
See him in there watching football,
Drinking beer and playing cards with Cousin Mel.
It's not Christmas without Grandma.
All the family's dressed in black,
And we just can't help but wonder:
Should we open up her gifts or send them back?

3. Now the goose is on the table,
And the pudding made of fig.
And the blue and silver candles,
That would just have matched the hair in Grandma's wig.
I've warned all my friends and neighbors.
Better watch out for yourselves.
They should never give a license
To a man who drives a sleigh and plays with elves.

Grandma's Killer Fruitcake

Words and Music by Elmo Shropshire and Rita Abrams

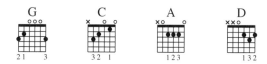

Intro
Country Polka

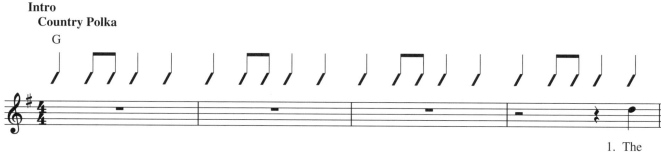

1. The
2., 3. *See Additional Lyrics*

Verse

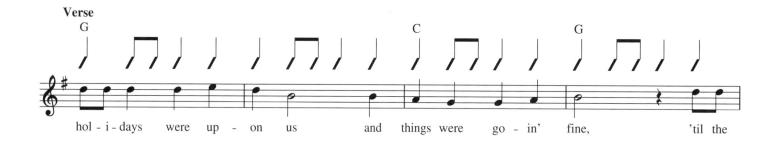

hol - i - days were up - on us and things were go - in' fine, 'til the

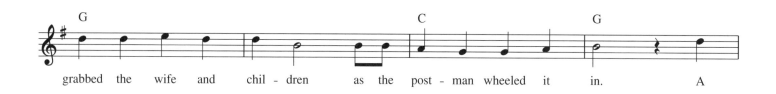

day I heard the door - bell and a chill ran up my spine. I

grabbed the wife and chil - dren as the post - man wheeled it in. A

year - ly Christ - mas night - mare has just come back a - gain. It was

Chorus

hard - er than the head of Un - cle Buck - y, heav - y as a Ser - mon of

Preach - er Luck - y. One's e - nough to give the whole state of Ken - tuck - y a

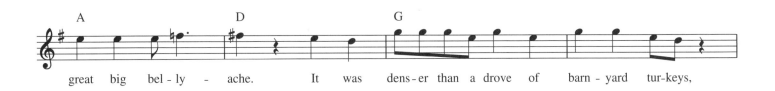

great big bel - ly - ache. It was dens - er than a drove of barn - yard tur - keys,

tough - er than a truck load of all beef jerk - y. Dri - er than a drought in

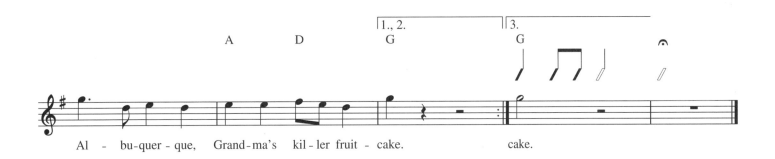

Al - bu - quer - que, Grand - ma's kil - ler fruit - cake. cake.

Additional Lyrics

2. Now I've had to swallow some marginal fare at our family feast.
   I even downed Aunt Dolly's possom pie just to keep the family peace.
   I winced at Wilma's gizzard mousse, but said it tasted fine,
   But that lethal weapon that Grandma bakes is where I draw the line.

3. It's early Christmas morning, the phone rings us awake.
   It's Grandma, Pa, she wants to know how'd we like the cake.
   "Well, Grandma, I never. Uh, we couldn't. It was, uh, unbelievable, that's for shore.
   What's that you say? Oh, no Grandma, Puh-leez don't send us more!"

The Greatest Gift of All

Words and Music by John Jarvis

Through the win - dow I ___ can see ___ snow be - gin to fall.

Know-ing you're in ___ love with me ___ is the great - est gift of ___ all.

Verse

3. Just be - fore I go to sleep _____ I hear a church bell ring.

Mer - ry Christ - mas ev - 'ry - one _____ is the song it ____ sings.

So I say a si - lent prayer ___ for crea - tures great and small.

Peace on earth good _ will to men is the great - est gift of ___ all. Peace on earth good _

will to men is the great - est gift of ___ all. _____

Last Christmas

Words and Music by George Michael

_____ love you." I meant it. Now __ I know __ what a fool _____ I've been. __ But if you

kissed me now __ I know you'd fool me a - gain. ___ fool me a - gain. ___

- cial. 3. A face on a lov - er with a fire in his heart, __ a

man un - der cov - er but you tore him a - part. __ May - be next year

I'll give it to some - one, I'll give it to some - one spe -

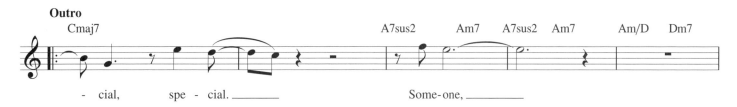

- cial, spe - cial. _____ Some-one, _____

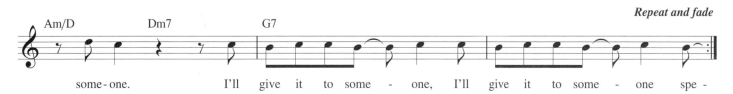

some - one. I'll give it to some - one, I'll give it to some - one spe -

Additional Lyrics

2. A crowded room, friends with tired eyes.
I'm hiding from you and your soul of ice.
My God, I thought you were someone to rely on.
Me, I guess I was a shoulder to cry on.
A face on a lover with a fire in his heart,
A man undercover but you tore me apart.
Ooh, now I've found a real love.
You'll never fool me again.

Lo, How a Rose E'er Blooming

15th Century German Carol
Translated by Theodore Baker
Music from *Alte Catholische Geistliche Kirchengesang*

Additional Lyrics

2. Isaiah 'twas foretold it,
   The rose I have in mind.
   With Mary we behold it,
   The Virgin Mother kind.
   To show God's love aright,
   She bore to men a Savior
   When half spent was the night.

Snowfall

Lyrics by Ruth Thornhill
Music by Claude Thornhill

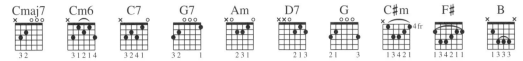

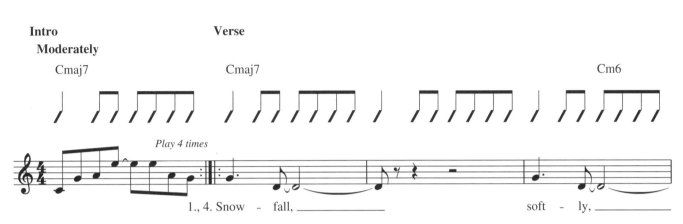

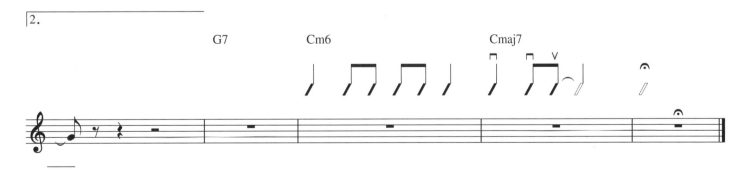

The Night Before Christmas Song

Music by Johnny Marks
Lyrics adapted by Johnny Marks from Clement Moore's Poem

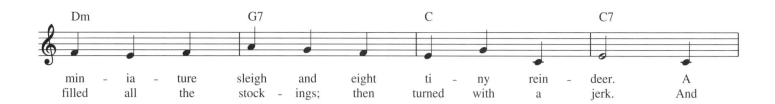

min - ia - ture sleigh and eight ti - ny rein - deer. A
filled all the stock - ings; then turned with a jerk. And

lit - tle old dri - ver so live - ly and quick, I
lay - ing his fin - ger a - side of his nose, then

knew in a mo - ment it must be St. Nick. 3. And more
giv - ing a nod up the chim - ney he rose; 6. But I

Verse

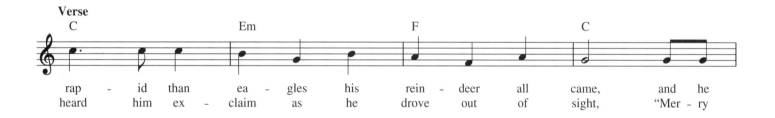

rap - id than ea - gles his rein - deer all came, and he
heard him ex - claim as he drove out of sight, "Mer - ry

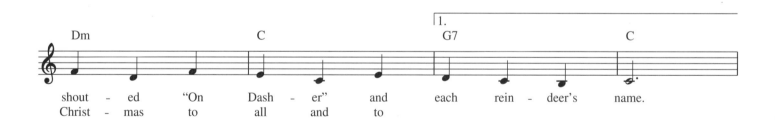

shout - ed "On Dash - er" and each rein - deer's name.
Christ - mas to all and to

4. And so all a good night!"

Parade of the Wooden Soldiers

English Lyrics by Ballard MacDonald
Music by Leon Jessel

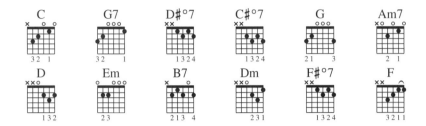

Verse
March Tempo

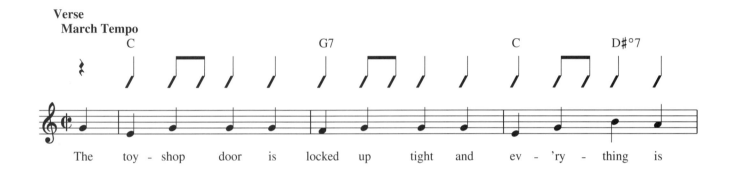

The toy - shop door is locked up tight and ev - 'ry - thing is

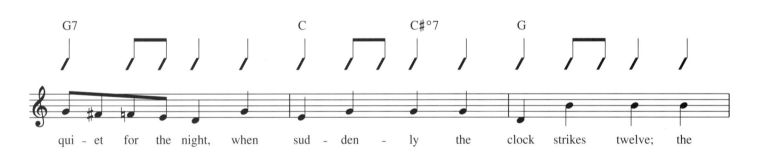

qui - et for the night, when sud - den - ly the clock strikes twelve; the

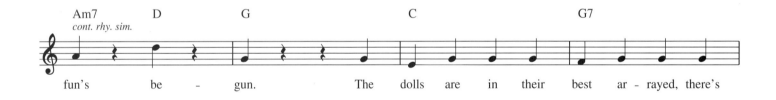

fun's be - gun. The dolls are in their best ar - rayed, there's

going to be a won - der - ful pa - rade. Hark to the drum, oh,

here they come, cries ev - 'ry - one!

Chorus

Hear them all cheer - ing, now they are near - ing, there's the cap - tain stiff as starch.

Bay - o - nets flash - ing, mu - sic is crash - ing as the wood - en sol - diers march.

Sa - bres a - click - ing, sol - diers a - wink - ing at each pret - ty lit - tle maid.

Here they come! Here they come! Here they come! Here they come! Wood - en sol - diers on pa - rade.

Day-light is creep - ing, dol - lies are sleep - ing in the toy - shop win - dow fast.

Sol - diers so jol - ly, think of each dol - ly dream - ing of the night that's past.

When in the morn - ing, with-out a warn - ing, toy - man pulls the win - dow shade,

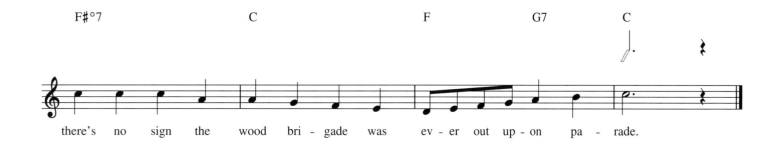

there's no sign the wood bri - gade was ev - er out up - on pa - rade.

Shake Me I Rattle
(Squeeze Me I Cry)

Words and Music by Hal Hackady and Charles Naylor

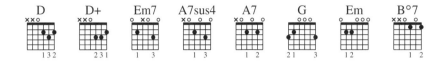

Intro
Moderately   **Verse**

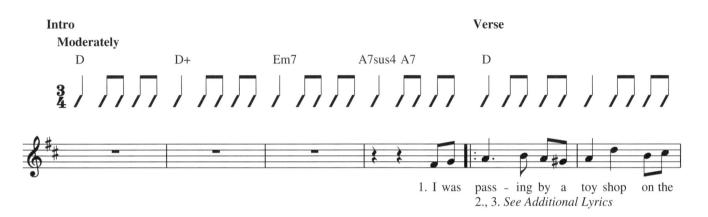

1. I was pass-ing by a toy shop on the
2., 3. *See Additional Lyrics*

cor — ner of the Square,   where a lit — tle girl was look — ing   in   the win-dow

cont. rhy. sim.

there.   She was look — ing at a dol — ly   in a   dress   of ros — y   red.   And a-

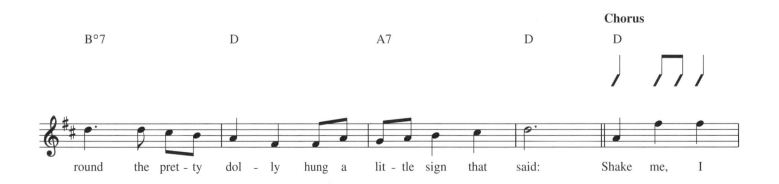

Chorus

round   the pret-ty dol — ly   hung a   lit — tle sign that   said: Shake   me,   I

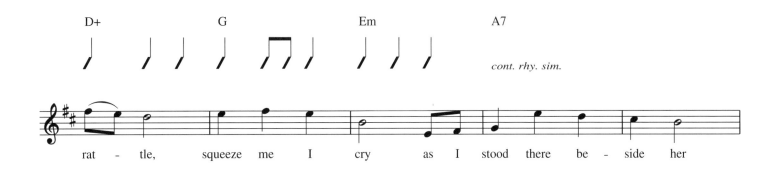

rat - tle, squeeze me I cry as I stood there be - side her

I could hear her sigh. Shake me I rat - tle, squeeze me I

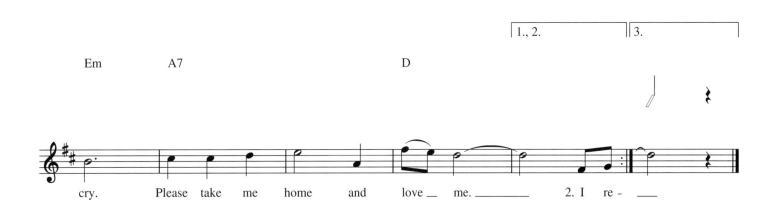

cry. Please take me home and love me. 2. I re -

Additional Lyrics

2. I recalled another toy shop on a square so long ago
   Where I saw a little dolly that I wanted so
   I remembered, I remembered how I longed to make it mine.
   And around that other dolly hung another little sign:

3. It was late and snow was falling as the shoppers hurried by,
   Past the girlie at the window with her little head held high.
   They were closing up the toy shop as I hurried through the door.
   Just in time to buy the dolly that her heart was longing for.

Toyland

Word by Glen MacDonough
Music by Victor Herbert

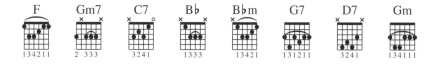

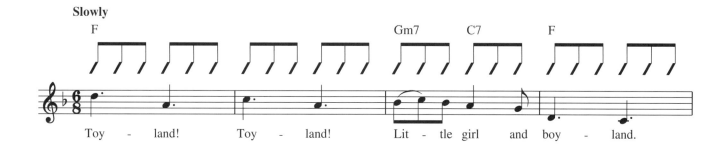

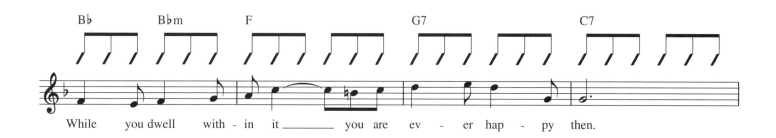

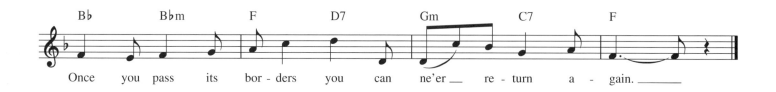

While Shepherds Watched Their Flocks

Words by Nahum Tate
Music by George Frideric Handel

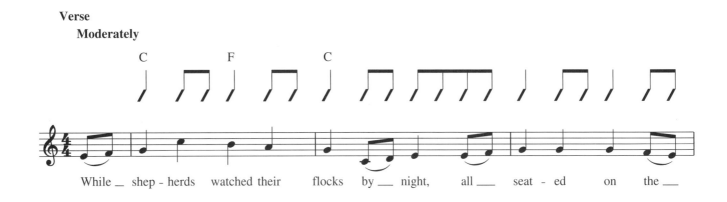

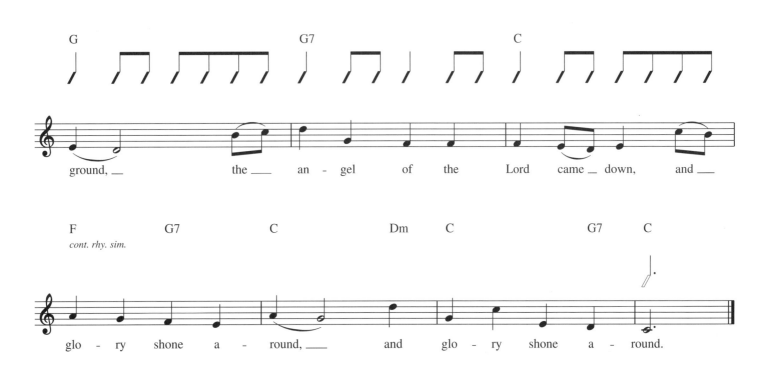

'Twas the Night Before Christmas

Words by Clement Clark Moore
Music by F. Henri Klickman

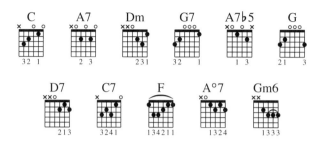

Verse
Brightly

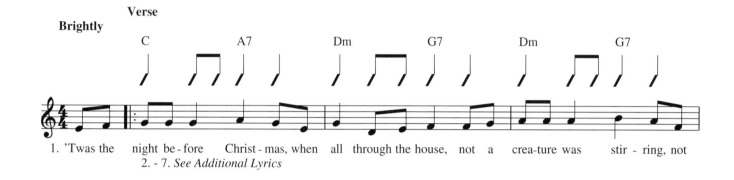

1. 'Twas the night be-fore Christ-mas, when all through the house, not a crea-ture was stir-ring, not
2. - 7. *See Additional Lyrics*

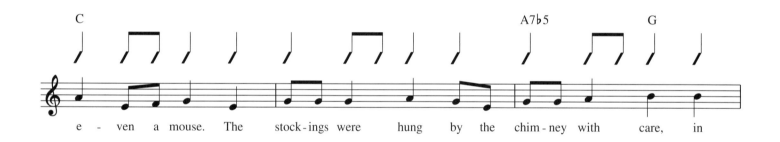

e - ven a mouse. The stock-ings were hung by the chim-ney with care, in

cont. rhy. sim.

hopes that Saint Nich-o-las soon would be there. The chil-dren were nest-led all

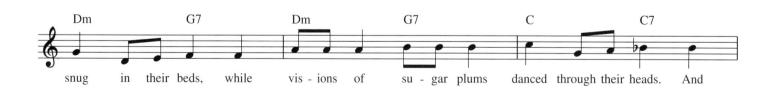

snug in their beds, while vis-ions of su-gar plums danced through their heads. And

Ma - ma   in   her   'ker - chief   and   I   in   my   cap,   had   just

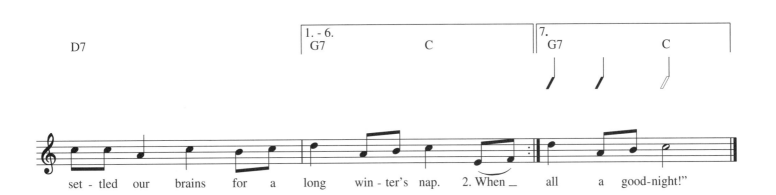

set - tled   our   brains   for   a   long   win - ter's   nap.   2. When __ all   a   good-night!"

Additional Lyrics

2. When out on the lawn there arouse such a clatter;
   I sprang from my bed to see what was the matter.
   Away to the window I flew like a flash,
   Tore open the shutters and threw up the sash.
   The moon, on the breast of the new-fallen snow,
   Gave a lustre of midday to objects below.
   When what to my wondering eyes should appear.
   But a miniature sleigh and eight tiny reindeer.

3. With a little old driver; so lively and quick,
   I knew in a moment it must be Saint Nick.
   More rapid than eagles, his coursers they came
   And he whistled, and shouted, and called them by name;
   "Now, Dasher, Now, Dancer! Now, Prancer! Now, Vixen!
   On Comet! On, Cupid! On Donder and Blitzen!
   To the top of the porch, to the top of the wall!
   Now dash away, dash away, dash away all!"

4. As dry leaves that before the wild hurricane fly,
   When they meet with an obstacle, mount to the sky.
   So up to the house-top the coursers they flew,
   With the sleigh full of toys, and Saint Nicholas, too.
   And then in a twinkling I heard on the roof
   The prancing and pawing of each little hoof.
   As I drew in my head, and was turning around,
   Down the chimney Saint Nicholas came with a bound.

5. He was dressed all in fir from his head to his foot
   And his clothes were all tarnished with ashes and soot.
   And he looked like a peddler just opening his pack.
   His eyes how they twinkled! His dimples how merry!
   His cheeks were like roses, his nose like a cherry,
   His droll little mouth was drawn up like a bow
   And the beard of his chin was as white as the snow.

6. The stump of a pipe he held tight in his teeth
   And the smoke, it encircled his head like a wreath.
   He had a broad face, and a round little belly
   That shook, when he laughed, like a bowl full of jelly.
   He was chubby and plump, a right jolly old elf,
   And I laughed when I saw him, in spite of myself.
   A wink of his eye and a twist of his head,
   Soon gave me to know I had nothing to dread.

7. He spoke not a word but went straight to his work,
   And filled all the stockings, then turned with a jerk,
   And laying his finger aside of his nose,
   And giving a nod, up the chimney he rose.
   He sprang to his sleigh, to his team gave a whistle
   And away they all flew like the down of a thistle,
   But I heard him exclaim, ere he drove out of sight:
   "Happy Christmas to all, and all a good-night!"

The Twelve Days of Christmas

Traditional English Carol

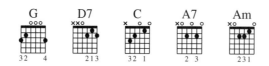

Verse
Moderately

1. On the first day of Christ-mas, my true love gave to me: a par-tridge _ in a pear

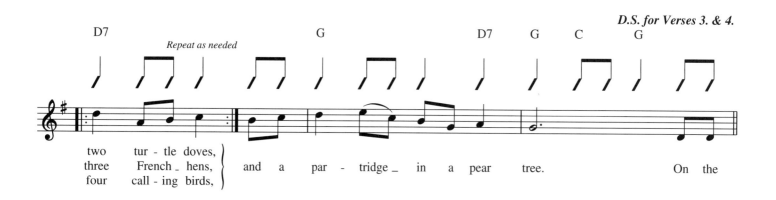

tree.
2. On the sec-ond day of Christ-mas, my true love sent to me:
3. third _ day of Christ-mas, my true love sent to me:
4. fourth _ day of Christ-mas, my true love sent to me:

D.S. for Verses 3. & 4.

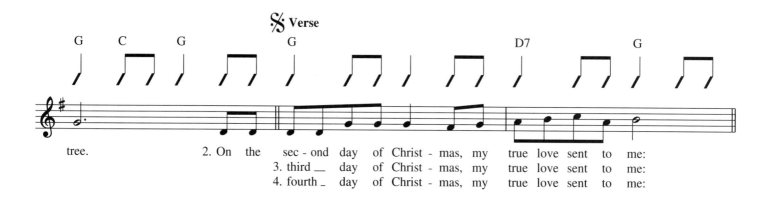

Repeat as needed

two tur-tle doves,
three French _ hens, and a par-tridge _ in a pear tree. On the
four call-ing birds,

Verse

5. fifth day of Christ-mas, my true love sent to me: five gold _____

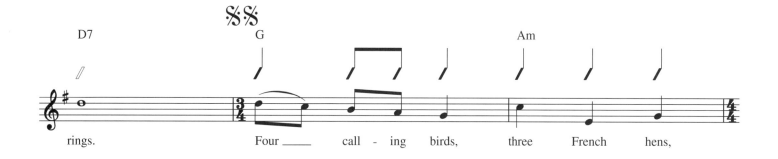

rings. Four ___ call - ing birds, three French hens,

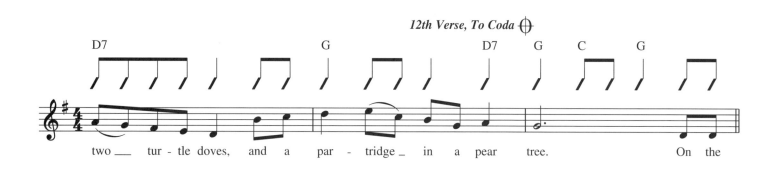

12th Verse, To Coda

two ___ tur - tle doves, and a par - tridge ___ in a pear tree. On the

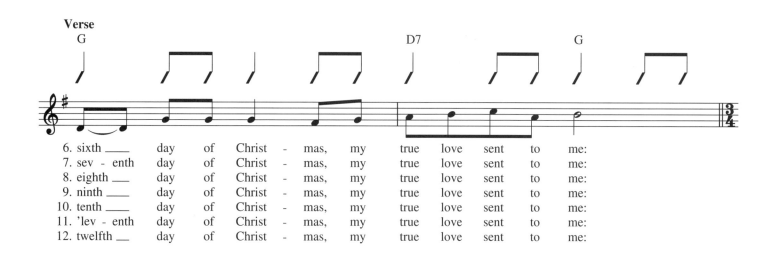

Verse

6. sixth ___ day of Christ - mas, my true love sent to me:
7. sev - enth day of Christ - mas, my true love sent to me:
8. eighth ___ day of Christ - mas, my true love sent to me:
9. ninth ___ day of Christ - mas, my true love sent to me:
10. tenth ___ day of Christ - mas, my true love sent to me:
11. 'lev - enth day of Christ - mas, my true love sent to me:
12. twelfth ___ day of Christ - mas, my true love sent to me:

D.S.S. for Verses 7. - 12.

Coda

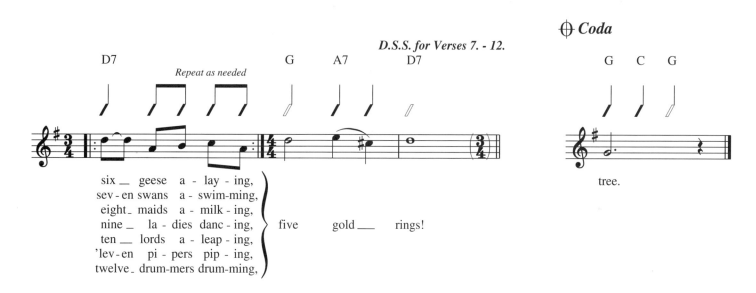

Repeat as needed

six ___ geese a - lay - ing,
sev - en swans a - swim - ming,
eight ___ maids a - milk - ing,
nine ___ la - dies danc - ing, } five gold ___ rings!
ten ___ lords a - leap - ing,
'lev - en pi - pers pip - ing,
twelve ___ drum - mers drum - ming,

tree.

217

We Need a Little Christmas

from MAME

Music and Lyric by Jerry Herman

Verse
Brightly

1. Haul out the hol - ly. _____ Put up the
2. *See Additional Lyrics*

tree be - fore my spir - it falls _____ a - gain.

cont. rhy. sim.

Fill up the stock - ing. _____ I may be

rush - ing things, but deck the halls _____ a - gain

now. _____

For we
3. For we

need a lit - tle Christ - mas, right this ver - y min - ute,
need a lit - tle mu - sic, need a lit - tle laugh - ter,

can - dles in the win - dow, car - ols at the spin - et. Yes, we
need a lit - tle sing - ing, ring - ing through the raft - er. And we

To Coda

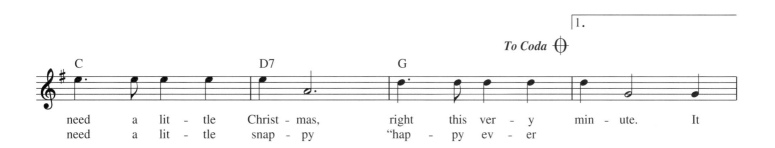

| 1.

need a lit - tle Christ - mas, right this ver - y min - ute. It
need a lit - tle snap - py "hap - py ev - er

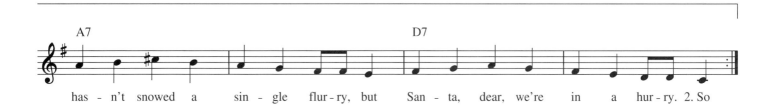

has - n't snowed a sin - gle flur - ry, but San - ta, dear, we're in a hur - ry. 2. So

| 2.

D.S. al Coda

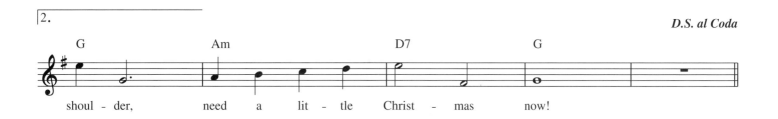

shoul - der, need a lit - tle Christ - mas now!

Coda

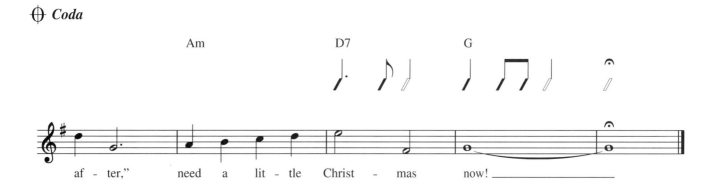

af - ter," need a lit - tle Christ - mas now! _____

Additional Lyrics

2. So climb down the chimney,
   Turn on the brightest string of lights I've ever seen.
   Slice up the fruitcake.
   It's time we hung some tinsel on the evergreen bough.
   For I've grown a little leaner, grown a little colder,
   Grown a little sadder, grown a little older,
   And I need a little angel, sitting on my shoulder,
   Need a little Christmas now!

You Make It Feel Like Christmas

Words and Music by Neil Diamond

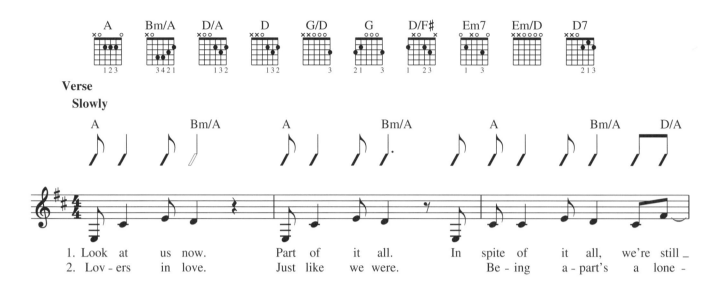

Verse

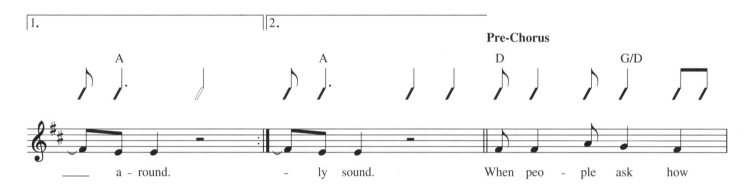

1. Look at us now. Part of it all. In spite of it all, we're still_
2. Lov - ers in love. Just like we were. Be - ing a - part's a lone -

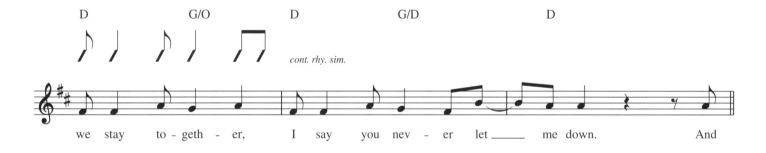

1. _ a - round.
2. Pre-Chorus - ly sound. When peo - ple ask how

cont. rhy. sim.

we stay to - geth - er, I say you nev - er let _ me down. And

Chorus

you make it feel _ like Christ - mas e - ven when things _ go _ wrong.

_ I hear the sound _ of Christ - mas in your song _

all year long.

Verse

3. Look at the sun shin - ing on me. No - where could be a bet -

Pre-Chorus

- ter place. Lov - ers in love. That's what we are.

Chorus

cont. rhy. sim.

Reach for that star out there ___ in space. 'Cause you make it feel ___ like Christ -

- mas e - ven when things ___ go ___ wrong. ___

I hear the sound ___ of Christ - mas in your song ___ all year

STRUM AND PICK PATTERNS

This chart contains the suggested strum and pick patterns that are referred to by number at the beginning
of each song in this book. The symbols ⊓ and ∨ in the strum patterns refer to down and up strokes, respectively.
The letters in the pick patterns indicate which right-hand fingers play which strings.

p = **thumb**
i = **index finger**
m = **middle finger**
a = **ring finger**

For example; Pick Pattern 2
is played: thumb - index - middle - ring

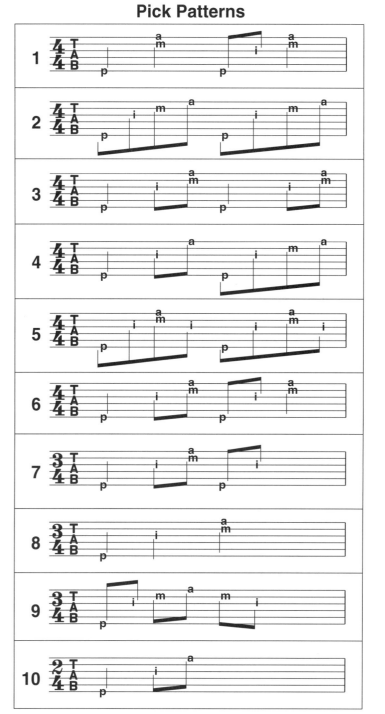

Strum Patterns   **Pick Patterns**

You can use the 3/4 Strum and Pick Patterns in songs written in compound meter (6/8, 9/8, 12/8, etc.).
For example, you can accompany a song in 6/8 by playing the 3/4 pattern twice in each measure.
The 4/4 Strum and Pick Patterns can be used for songs written in cut time (¢) by doubling the note
time values in the patterns. Each pattern would therefore last two measures in cut time.

STRUM IT GUITAR LEGEND

Strum It is the series designed especially to get you playing (and singing!) along with your favorite songs. The idea is simple – the songs are arranged using their original keys in lead sheet format, providing you with the authentic chords for each song, beginning to end. Rhythm slashes are written above the staff. Strum the chords in the rhythm indicated. Use the chord diagrams found at the top of the first page of the arrangement for the appropriate chord voicings. The melody and lyrics are also shown to help you keep your spot and sing along.

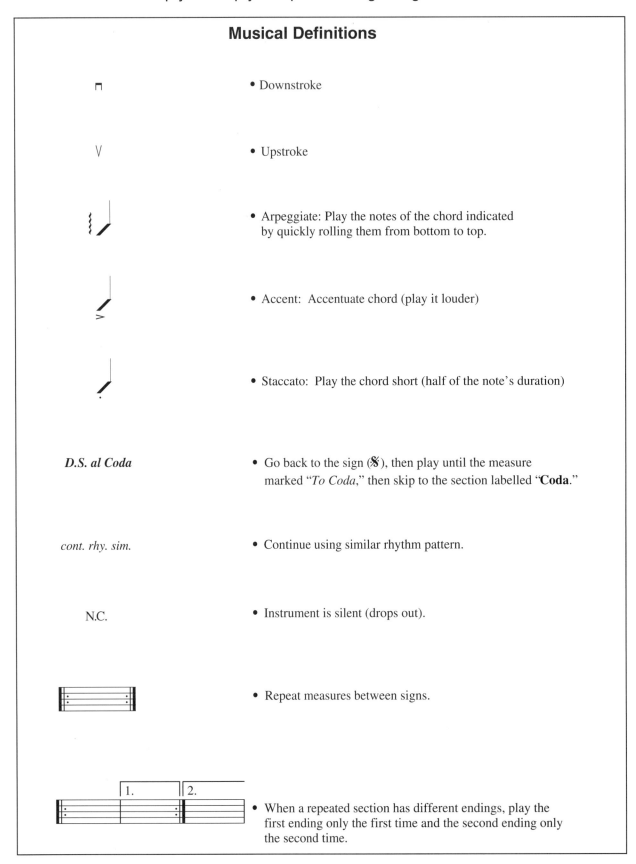

Musical Definitions

- Downstroke

- Upstroke

- Arpeggiate: Play the notes of the chord indicated by quickly rolling them from bottom to top.

- Accent: Accentuate chord (play it louder)

- Staccato: Play the chord short (half of the note's duration)

D.S. al Coda
- Go back to the sign (𝄋), then play until the measure marked "*To Coda*," then skip to the section labelled "**Coda**."

cont. rhy. sim.
- Continue using similar rhythm pattern.

N.C.
- Instrument is silent (drops out).

- Repeat measures between signs.

- When a repeated section has different endings, play the first ending only the first time and the second ending only the second time.